Catherine Curry Cobham

Recipes From

1700's - 1800's

Disclaimer

In compiling the information and facts in this book, reliance is based on documents, letters that are in my possession, most of them came to me through my husband's mother Constance Clark Hurlbut, who spent her early years at Cobham Park. It is not my intent to take credit for any original, artistic creativity, or information included in this book

Jacqueline F. Hurlbut.
July 4 2014

Copyright © 2014 by **Cobham Design**
All rights reserved. This book or any portion thereof
may not be reproduced or used in any manner whatsoever
without the express written permission of the publisher
except for the use of brief quotations in a book review.
Printed in the United States of America

First Printing, **2014**

ISBN-13: 978-0692254455   ISBN-10: 0692254455

Create Space

https://www.createspace.com/

Dedication

To a wonderful extended family that lived through culinary
disasters, survived, and yes felt free to laugh at the experience.
To Three Amazing Children,
Beloved son David, who supported each endeavor,
Precious Daughter Danielle who learned at a young age to make a
perfect cup of tea to calm calamity, in the kitchen.
Equally precious Daughter Kirsten who at 6 years of age after
dinner one evening, said
"Mama you have to put Hamburger Meat in Hamburger Helper",
(One of those silly little things, I forgot)
And to my Magnificent Grandchildren,
Christian, Chase, Savannah, and Lily Grace who show
unconditional love toward me, with or without cooking skills but
compliment me on fine table settings and tell me how well I
decorate the family Christmas tree,
Finally to David
Whose ancestor is the real author of this book?

Table of Contents

Acknowledgment 9
Green Mountain Cake 17
Crisp Paste for Fruit Tarts and Minced Pies 19
Rich Short Past 21
Mrs. Cobham's Jelly 23
Mrs. C Blancmange 25
Currant Wine 27
Sanbridge Pancakes 29
Newcastle Pudding 31
Farmer's Apple Pudding 33
Approved Jumble 35
Fruit Cake 37
To Make Good Starch 39
Pickled Cucumbers 41
Lemon Pies 43
Spiced Beef 45
Pain de Pomme 47
Force Meat Steak 49
Minced Meat Fritters 51
Ginger Pound Cake 53
Buckwheat Cakes 55
Ginger Bread 57
Lemon Cheese Cakes 61
Scotch Short Cake 63
Soft Ginger Bread 65
Potato Pie 67
Clove Cake 69
Carolina Cake 69
Scotch Loaf 71
Washington Cake 73
College Pudding 75
Palo Alto Cakes 77
Yellow Lady Cake 79
White Lady Cake 83
Lemon Pudding 87
Muffins 89
To Make Primo Vinegar 91
Sponge Cake 93
Cup Cake 95

To Make a Corn Cake worth Eating	95
A Recipe for Making Hot Cross Buns	97
Artificial Oysters	99
To Make A Venison Pasty	101
Mr. Henry's Recipe for Curing Ham, Pork or Beef	103
Mr. Page's Recipe for Beef	103
To Make Cheesecake	105
A Recipe for Gingerbread	107
A Very Excellent Pudding	109
Maccaroni	111
A Maccaroni Pudding	113
Corn Bread	115
The French Pot au Feu or National Soup of France	117
Wedding Cake	119
Pork Sausage of a Very Superior Flavor & Quality	121
To Make Sealing Wax	123
Soft Ginger Bread	125
Portable Lemonade	125
Gateau de Pommes	127
Rice Cup Pudding	129
For the Hair	131
Scotch Loaf	133
Quince Jelly	135
Scotch Loaf	137
To Cure Hams	139
Grape Wine, Simple & Perfect	141
Scotch Short Bread	143
Soda Biscuit	145
Short Biscuit	145
To Make a Bread Pudding	147
Corn Fritters	149
Varnish for Colored Drawings	151
To Mend Iron Pots	151
Dover Cake	153
Apple or Gooseberry Soufflé	155
To Color Green	157
Culinary Measurements	182
Short Histories of Culinary Functions	186
Glossary	191

Acknowledgements

Margaret Lawson.
Keeper of so many documents that she lovingly shared, along with information handed down from previous generations.

Suzanne LeMehaute Photography
Hilton Head Island SC 29928
www.SoozStudio.com
A free spirit artist.

Mike Dillard.
dillardma@yahoo.com
A book cover and idea guy, always there, fabulous artist and cartoonist.

Shutter Stock Border Art.

Various information garnered from the Internet i.e. Wikipedia and conversations with people who were familiar with cooking tables, ingredients, and utensils of days gone by.
Thank you.

Lancashire Rose

Catherine Curry Cobham was the wife of George Ashworth Cobham, Sr. they married October 27 1828 in Lancashire England. After residing in Paris and Le Havre, France for several years, the family finally immigrated to America. George Ashworth, Sr. and Elizabeth Cobham resided in Warren, Pennsylvania until their deaths. Catherine was the Mother of Henry Cobham, born January 24 1824, Brigadier General George Ashworth Cobham Jr. born December 5 1825, Frederick Fearns Cobham born September 7 1831, (died May 21 1835.) all her sons were born in England. Her daughter Georgina Cobham was born in France March 20 1834. Her youngest daughters were born in the United States of America daughters Elizabeth Cobham on April 11 1837 and Alice Cobham on June 19 1839.

Catherine, noted for her entertaining and grand parties at Cobham Park, Warren, Pennsylvania kept her recipes in several small books. Many of her culinary delights were those that she created as a young woman and family recipes from England and France along with those that she fashioned and shaped in America. Her table settings were of the utmost elegance; no doubt a continuance from Fearnes Hall in England and her entertaining in France.

Her recipes were all hand written and great care has been taken to copy them as faithfully as possible. These recipe books have been passed down and used through the generations and at this time are in the possession of Margaret Lawson and myself.

Many of the terms, she referred to are from Europe. She used European utensils that she brought with her to her adopted home; fortunately, we still possess many of them. My children loved to use the cookie cutters and the butter moulds; it was never a problem to have butter moulds at all the holiday occasions. I have to admit they did exceedingly well and when invited to a celebration or gathering often took them as host gifts, much to the delight of their host.

In earlier times, certain phrases were used in the preparation of food; we have tried to capture those phrases along with an explanation. A perfect example is "the washing of butter." When I first read the terminology I was mystified, but it is true "they washed butter." Many ingredients are unknown in the cooking world today. One is "Isinglass" used very often in the preparation of jellies, the dying of material and numerous other uses.

On this journey to prepare, and understand her recipes, I encountered surprising culinary experiences and information gained from exploring terms, descriptions, origins, along with a completely new respect and admiration of the women of that period. What they had to accomplish from beginning to end in order to prepare foods and run households along with showing care and concern for their families was truly inspiring.

One cannot forget how hard the work was of those who were employed as domestic help. Yes, it is true that we work hard today but the work of today's homemaker (a worthy profession) is very different. Moreover, while we have to contend with so much more in our daily living, the chores of days gone by were long and tedious; commanding devotion and attention to so many things we take for granted.

We have made copies of her original recipe books, which reflect very old and tired pages. Although her writing is legible, we have typed the recipes to give clarity to those who will enjoy trying out these tried and true delectables.

No changes to her spelling have been made and what appear to be incorrect punctuations have been left in place. I imagined her to be so busy in the preparation of food that she jotted down information as she went along. Notably some recipes are written in faultless long hand and as she aged, others have a lesser perfection. To change these recipes to meet ideal writing skills and terms would take away from the authenticity of her work.

In many instances, she referred to a pinch of this or a nickel of that; we have included tables to show those measurements. No oven temperatures were included in her writings. At the time she was creating her recipes; ovens were not equipped as they are today. The baking heat was a fine art and very much part of being a good cook. One did not leave the kitchen or oven while food was being prepared, unlike today when we can set a timer or set a pre timer and walk away to immerse ourselves in other activities.

Catherine Curry Cobham was truly devoted to her family. The stories handed down to us in writings from Henry, George, Georgina, Elizabeth, and Alice along with the writings of the English relatives that visited, tell of celebrations, delightful parties, along with superb food, and of course dancing in the ballroom; all at the hands of Catherine, albeit with domestic help. Of course, throughout all of these functions she was in her element as a Grand Hostess.

Catherine Curry Cobham loved flowers and always maintained a cutting garden so that she would have fresh flowers. This was no doubt a carry over from England where cutting gardens were and are a way of life. We have chosen to decorate her recipes with flowers as a tribute to her.

Our hope is you will enjoy the contents of this recipe book along with the blank art pages that we designed for you to write some of your own tried and true creations that you can leave for future generations.

Bon Appetite.

Green Mountain Cake
1 Egg, 1 cup white Sugar
1 cup of Milk, 1 Teaspoonful
Cream of Tartar to be mixed in
two Tea cups of Flour, half teaspoon
of Soda dissolved in the Milk
and one teaspoonful Essence
of Lemon

Green Mountain Cake

1 Egg, 1 cup of white Sugar
1 cup of Milk, 1 Teaspoonful
Cream Of Tartar to be mixed in two
Teacups of flour,
half a teaspoon of Soda dissolved in the
milk, and one teaspoonful of Essence of
Lemon.

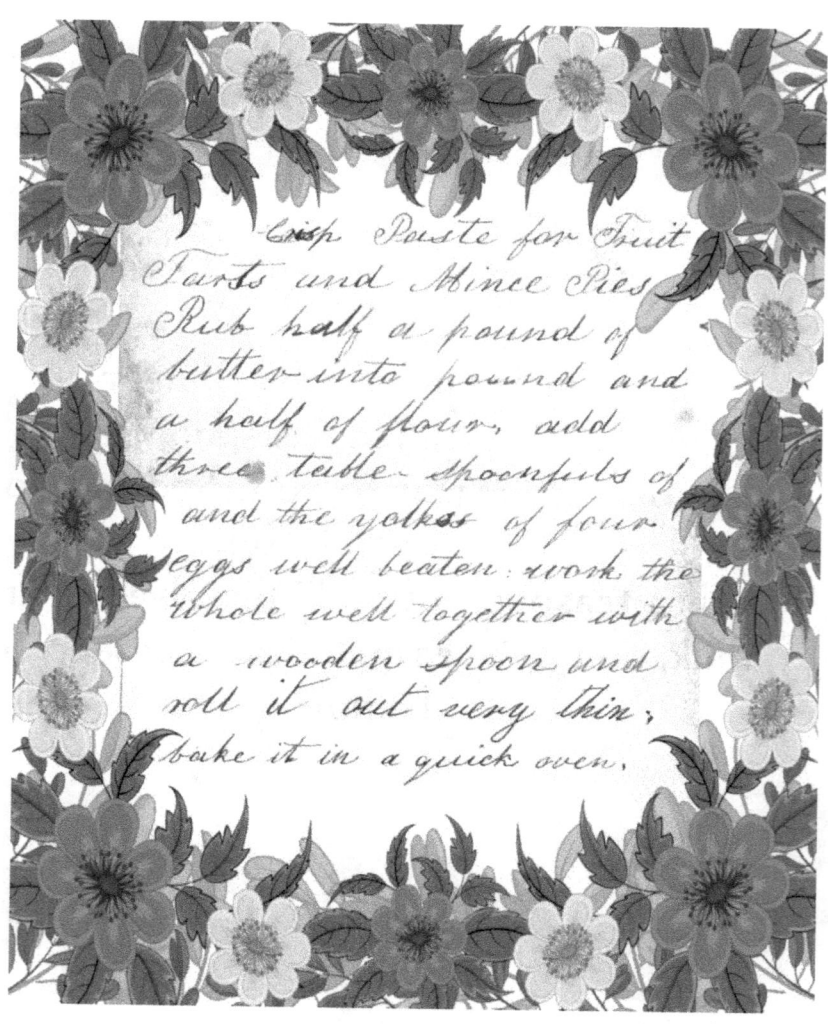

Crisp Paste for Fruit Tarts and Mince Pies. Rub half a pound of butter into pound and a half of flour, add three table spoonfuls of and the yolks of four eggs well beaten: work the whole well together with a wooden spoon and roll it out very thin; bake it in a quick oven.

Crisp Paste for Fruit Tarts and Mince Pies

Rub half a pound of Butter into pound and
half of flour
add three table spoons of
powdered sugar and
the yolks of four eggs
well beaten: work the whole well together
with a wooden spoon and roll it out very
thin; bake it in a quick oven.

A Rich Short Past.
Equal quantities of flour, butter, and pounded sugar rub the butter with the flour and mix in the sugar, rubbing the whole together till it will roll out to about half an inch in thickness.

Rich Short Past

Equal quantities of flower butter and pounded sugar rub the butter with the flour and mix in the sugar, rubbing the whole together till it will roll out to about half an inch in thickness.

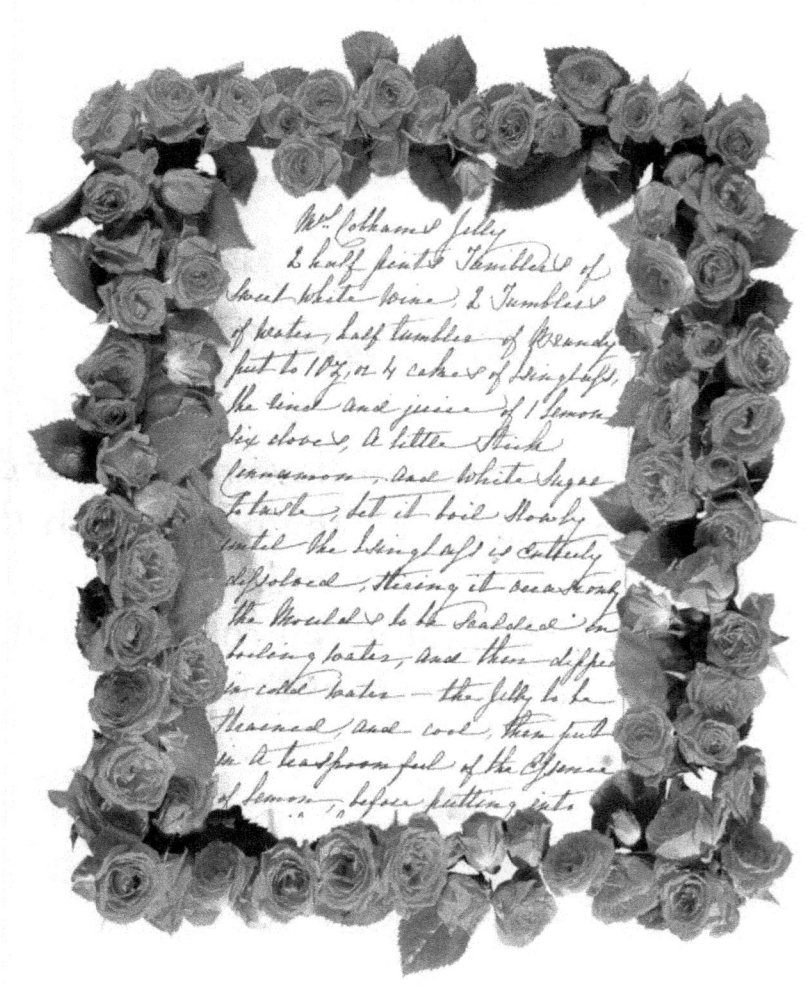

Mrs Cotham's Jelly

2 half pint Tumblers of
Sweet White wine, 2 Tumblers
of water, half tumbler of Brandy,
put to 1 oz, or 4 cakes of Isinglass,
the rind and juice of 1 Lemon
Six cloves, A little Stick
Cinnamon — and White Sugar
to taste, let it boil slowly
until the Isinglass is entirely
dissolved, stirring it occasionally
the Moulds to be Scalded in
boiling water, and then dipped
in cold water — the Jelly to be
Strained, and cool, then put
in A teaspoon ful of the Essence
of Lemon, before putting into

Mrs. Cobhams Jelly

2 half pints tumblers of sweet white wine, 2 tumblers of water, half a tumbler of Brandy put to 10 oz or 4 cakes of Isinglass, the rind and juice of 1 Lemon, six cloves, a little stick of Cinnamon and white sugar to taste, let it boil slowly until the Isinglass is entirely dissolved, stirring it occasionally. The moulds to be scalded in boiling water, and then dipped in cold water. The jelly, to be strained, and cool then put in a teaspoonful of the Essence of Lemon before putting into Moulds.

Mrs C— Blancmange

To 1½ ozs of Isinglass add five tumblers full of new Milk, a little stick Cinnamon, the peel of a lemon, and white Sugar to taste, let it boil slowly, stirring all the time until the Isinglass is completely dissolved, then strain thro' a fine sieve, and stir until cool, then add two teaspoonfuls of Essence of lemon and two of Extract of Bitter Almonds —
The Moulds prepared as for Jelly

Mrs. C- Blancmange

To 10 oz of Isinglass add 5 tumblers full of new milk, A little stick of Cinnamon, the Peel of a lemon, and white sugar to taste. let it boil slowly, stirring all the time until the isinglass is completely dissolved, then strain this through a fine sieve, and stand until cool, then add two teaspoonfuls of essence of lemons and two of extract of bitter almonds-
The moulds prepared as for Jelly.

Currant Wine

To one quart of ripe Currans juice add 3 pounds. of the very best white sugar, the finer the quality the better. and to this add as much water as will with the juice and sugar make a gallon. Put the mixture into a keg or demijohn leaving it open for two weeks, or untill the fermentation subsides; then cork up tightly, and let it remain quiet, for five months, when it will be fit for use,

Currant Wine

To one quart of ripe Currant juice add 3 pounds of the very best white sugar, the finer the quality the better and to this add as much water as will, with the juice and sugar make a gallon. Put the mixture in a keg or demijohn leaving open for two weeks, or until the fermentation subsides; then cork up tightly, and let it remain quiet for five months, when it will be fit for use.

Sanbridge Pancakes

Beat four Eggs, with four Tablespoonfuls of Flour, with a little Nutmeg, and Salt, half pint of Milk, ¼ lb Butter melted into it, when nearly cold, mix all together with one ounce of Sugar, warm the pan over the fire, and put in a sufficient quantity of the Batter to make a very thin Pancake, without any fat to fry them in, and only fry one side, strew Sugar between them, and place the brown side uppermost

Sanbridge Pancakes

Beat four eggs with four Tablespoons of flour with a little nutmeg, and salt, half pint of milk ¼ lb of butter melted into it, when nearly cold mix all together with one ounce of sugar, warm the pan over the fire, and put in a sufficient quantity of the batter to make a very thin Pancake, without any fat to fry them in, and only fry one side, Strew sugar between them, and place the brown side uppermost.

Newcastle Pudding

Make a custard of 6 Eggs
to 1 quart of Milk, and Sugar
to taste; beat the Eggs, stir them
in the Milk, then add the Sugar,

Butter some bread, lay it in
the bottom of a dish, then strew
over it some currants, then another
layer of buttered bread and
currants, pour on the Egg & Milk
prepared as above, and bake
until the custard is thick

Newcastle Pudding

Make a custard of 6 eggs to a quart of Milk, and Sugar to taste; beat the eggs, stir them in the milk, then add the sugar. Butter some bread, lay it in the bottom of a dish, then strew over it some currants, then another layer of buttered bread, pour on the egg and milk as prepared above, and bake until the custard is thick.

Former's Apple Pudding

Stew some tender apples, if they should be juicy, they will require very little water to cook them; add to one pound of mashed Apples, whilst hot, a quarter of a pound of butter, and sugar to the taste. beat your eggs and stir in when the Apple is cold.

Butter the bottom and sides of a deep pudding dish, strew it very thickly with bread crumbs, put in the Mixture, and strew bread crumbs plentifully over the top, set it in a tolerably hot oven, and when baked till brown over — This is good with

Farmers Apple Pudding

Stew some tender apples, if they should be juicy, they will require very little water to cook them; add to one pound of mashed apples, whilst hot a quarter pound of butter, and sugar to the taste. Beat 4 eggs and stir in when the apple is cold, Butter the bottom and sides of a deep pudding dish, strew it very thickly with bread crumbs, put in the mixture, and strew breadcrumbs plentifully over the top, set it in a tolerably hot oven, and when baked, sift sugar over.
This is good with a glass of rich milk.

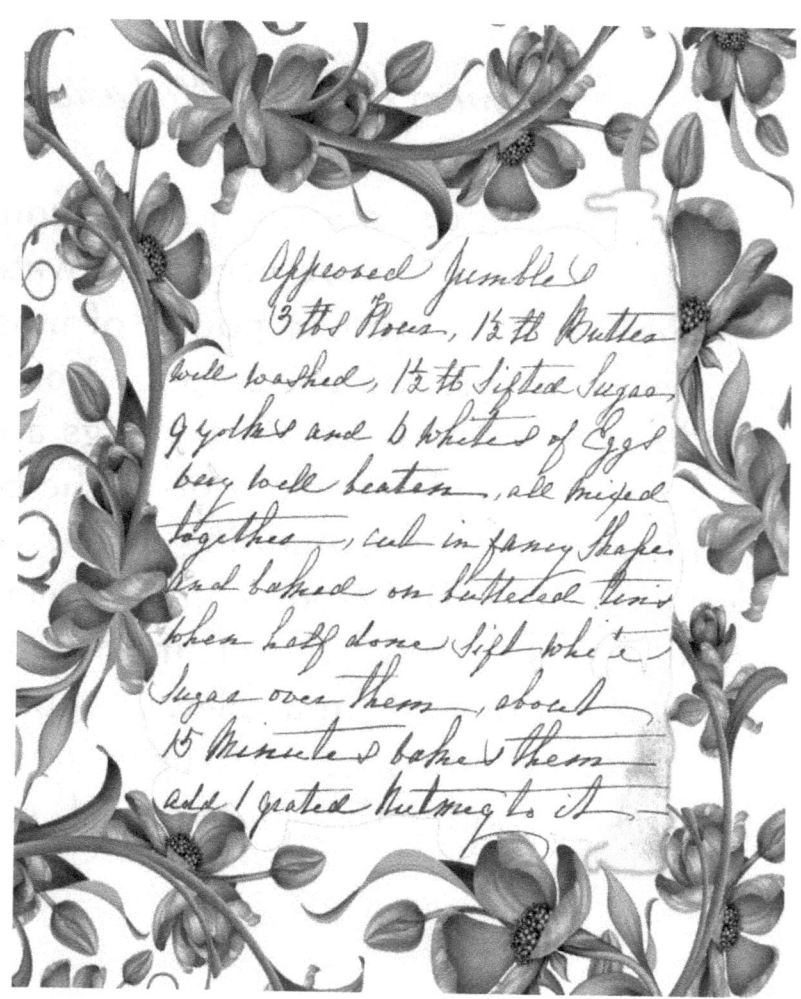

Approved Jumble

3 lbs Flour, 1½ lb Butter well washed, 1½ lb Sifted Sugar, 9 yolks and 6 whites of Eggs being well beaten, all mixed together, cut in fancy Shapes and baked on buttered tins when half done Sift white Sugar over them, about 15 Minutes bakes them add 1 grated Nutmeg to it

Approved Jumble

3 lbs flour, 1 ½ lbs Butter well washed, 1 ½ lbs sifted sugars, 9 yolks and 6 whites of eggs very well beaten, all mixed together, cut in fancy shapes and baked in buttered tins, when half done sift white sugar over them, about 15 minutes bake them add 1 grated nutmeg to it.

Fruit Cake

1 lb of Flour, 1 lb Sugar
¾ lb Butter well washed,
and 10 Eggs – beat the Butter
to a cream, then add the
Sugar, then the yolks of ten
Eggs well beaten, then the
Flour, 1 grated Nutmeg, Some
Mace & cloves, and then the
Whites beaten to a high froth
have ready 1½ lbs Raisins,
2 lbs Currants, 1 lb cut citron
& half Pint of Brandy, Strew
over the currants 2 oz More
flour, when well mixed
add two teaspoonfuls of
finely powdered Saleratus
dissolved in a little vinegar
paper the Tins, and put the
mixture in two inches thick
bake in a moderate oven

Fruit Cake

1 lb of flour, 1lb of sugar, ¾ lb of Butter well washed, and 10 eggs- beat the butter to a cream then add the sugar, then the yolks of ten eggs well beaten, then the flour, 1 grated nutmeg, some mace and cloves, and the whites beaten to a high froth, have ready 1 1/2lbs of raisins 2lbs of currants 1lb cut citron 2 half pint of brandy, strewn over the currants, 2oz more of flour, when well mixed add two teaspoonful's of finely powdered Celeratus dissolved in a little vinegar. Paper the tins and put the mixture in two inches thick bake in a moderate oven.

To make good Starch
2 oz of fine white gum
Arabic powder, put into a Jug
and pour on it a pint of boiling
water, cover and let stand all
Night, then Strain into a Bottle
corked close to keep for use —
A Table Spoonful put
to a pint of Starch made
in the usual will give to
Lawns, White or Printed, a
look of Newness, when nothing
else can restore them — after
washing — It is also good
(much diluted) for thin white
Muslin and lace

To make good Starch

2oz of fine white gum Arabic powder pour it in a jug and pour on it a pint of boiling water, cover and let stand all night, then strain into a bottle corked close to keep for use. A tablespoon put to a pint of starch made in the usual will give to lawns, white or printed a look of newness, when nothing else can restore them after washing, It is also good (much diluted) for thin white Muslin and Lace.

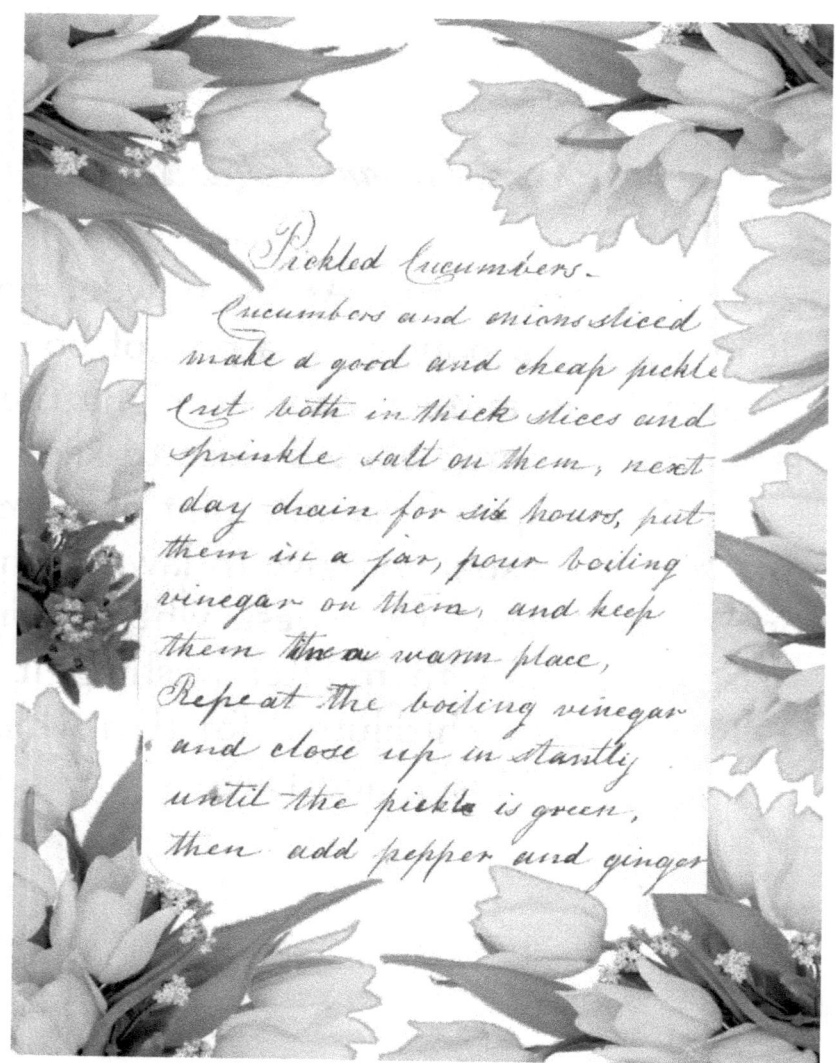

Pickled Cucumbers.

Cucumbers and onions sliced make a good and cheap pickle. Cut both in thick slices and sprinkle salt on them, next day drain for six hours, put them in a jar, pour boiling vinegar on them, and keep them in a warm place, Repeat the boiling vinegar and close up instantly until the pickle is green, then add pepper and ginger

Pickled Cucumbers

Cucumbers and onions sliced make a good a cheap pickle. Cut both in thick slices and sprinkle salt on them, next day drain for six hours, put them in a jar, pour boiling vinegar over them and keep them in a warm place. Repeat the boiling vinegar and close up instantly until the pickle is green then add pepper and ginger.

Lemon Pies —
Grate the peels of four lemons, and squeeze the juice into the grated peels. Then take nine eggs, leaving out half of the whites, one pound of loaf (or white) sugar, half a pound of butter, one pint of cream (or of milk). add four table spoonfulls of rose water, and beat them well together, and add the lemon. Divide into four pies, with under crust

Lemon Pies

Grate the peels of four lemons and squeeze the juice into the grated peels. Then take nine eggs leaving out half of the whites, one pound of loaf (or white) sugar half a pound of butter, one pint of cream(or of milk) add four tablespoons of rose water and beat them well together, and add the lemon. Divide into four pies with under crust and bake.

Spiced Beef.

For twelve pounds of the round, rump, or thick flank of beef, take a large teaspoonful of freshly pounded mace, the same of ground black pepper, twice as much of cloves, one small nutmeg and a quarter of a teaspoonful of good cayenne, all in the finest powder. Mix them well with seven ounces of brown sugar, rub the beef with this, and let it lie three days. Then add half a pound of fine salt, rub and turn it once in twelve days, just wash it, but not soak it; skewer and bind it into good form, put it in a stew pan of nearly its own size, pour to it a pint and half of good beef broth, and when it begins to boil skim and throw in one small onion, a bunch of thyme and parsley, and two or three carrots. Let it simmer softly for four hours and a half. If wanted cold, leave it to stand in the gravy. This far surpasses corned beef.

Spiced Beef

For twelve pounds of the round rump or thick flank of beef take a large teaspoonful of freshly pounded mace, the same of black pepper, twice as much of cloves, one small nutmeg and a quarter of a teaspoonful of good cayenne, all in the finest powders. Mix them well with seven ounces of brown sugar, rub the beef with this, and let it lie for three days. Then add ½ pound of fine salt and turn it once in twenty-four hours for twelve days. Just wash it, but not swell it; skewer and bind it into good form, put it in a stew pan of nearly its own size, pour to it a pint and a half of good beef broth, and when it begins to boil skim and throw in one small onion, a bunch of thyme and parsley, and two or three carrots. Let it simmer softly for Four and Half hours, if wanted cold leave it to stand in the gravy. This far surpasses corned beef.

Pain de Pomme:
Boil a dozen dumpling apples till they are soft; peel and core them, break them up, and force the pulp through a coarse sive. mix this with twice its weight of dough. make the whole into small ~~loaves~~, and bake in a slow oven.

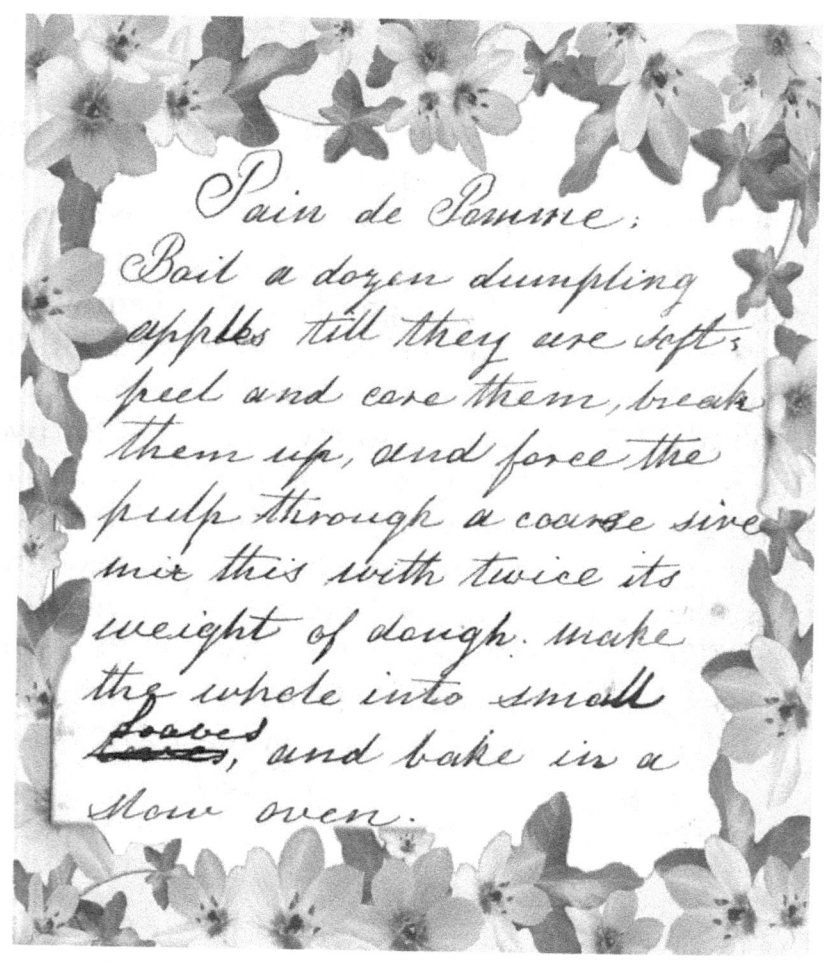

Pain de Pomme

Boil a dozen dumpling apples till they are soft, peel and core them, break them up, and force the pulp through a coarse sive mix this with twice its weight of dough, make the whole into small loaves and bake in a slow oven.

Force Meat Steak —

A Large thick slice from the middle of the rump of beef, when tender, makes an excellent small make a roll of force meat, place this in the steak, roll it up tight, cover with a buttered paper, and roast it an hour and a half or more, according to size. Twenty minutes before it is served take off the paper and flour the meat, which should be kept well basted with butter all the time it is roasting. Serve up with brown gravy.

Force Meat Steak

A large thick steak from the middle of the rump of beef, when tender makes an excellent small dish of roast meat, make a roll of forcemeat, place this in the steak, roll it up tight, cover with a buttered paper, and roast it an hour and a half or more according to size. Twenty minutes before it is served take off the paper and flour the meat, which should be kept well basted with butter all the time it is roasting, serve up with brown gravy.

Mince Meat Fitters.

With half a pound of mince meat mix four ounces of fine breadcrumbs, or a tablespoonful of flour, two eggs well beaten, and the strained juice of half a lemon, mix these well, and drop the fritters with a dessert spoon into plenty of very hot lard or fresh butter fry them seven or eight minutes, drain on a napkin and send them very hot to table. These Fritters should be quite small.

Mince Meat Fritters

With a half a pound of mince meat mix two ounces of fine breadcrumbs, or a tablespoonful of flour, two eggs well beaten, and the strained juice of half a lemon; mix these well and drop the fritters with a dessert spoon into plenty of very pure lard or fresh butter, fry them seven or eight minutes; drain on a napkin, and send them very hot to the table. These fritters should be quite small.

Ginger Pound Cake.
Three quarters of a pound of
Butter. Three quarters of a
pound of sugar. Six eggs. one
pound and a half of flour;
one pint of molasses. the
grated rind of two large
oranges. Three tablespoonfuls
of ginger, two table spoonfuls
of Cinnamon. one table spoon
ful. of dissolved salaeratus
or one large teaspoonful
of dissolved carbonate of
ammonia. Beat the butter
and sugar to a cream.
Beat the eggs very light
and add to it, then stir in

except the salaeratus or
ammonia. Beat the mixture
very hard for several minutes
then stir in the salaeratus
or ammonia. Butter an
earthen cake mould, a thick
iron pan, pour in the mixture
and bake in a moderate
oven. If you bake it in an
iron pan line the pan with
several thicknesses of stout
paper well buttered ——

Ginger Pound Cake

Three quarters of a pound of Butter, Three quarters of a pound of sugar; six eggs; one pound and a half of flour, one pint of molasses; the grated rind of two large oranges; Three tablespoonfuls of ginger two tablespoonfuls of Cinnamon; one tablespoonful of salaeratus or one large teaspoonful of carbonate of ammonia. Beat the butter and sugar to a cream. Beat the eggs very light and add to it; then mix in all the other ingredients except the salaeratus or ammonia. Beat the mixture very hard for several minutes then stir in the salaeratus or ammonia. Butter an earthen cake mould or thick iron pan, pour in the mix. If you bake it in an iron pan line the pan with several thicknesses of stout paper well buttered

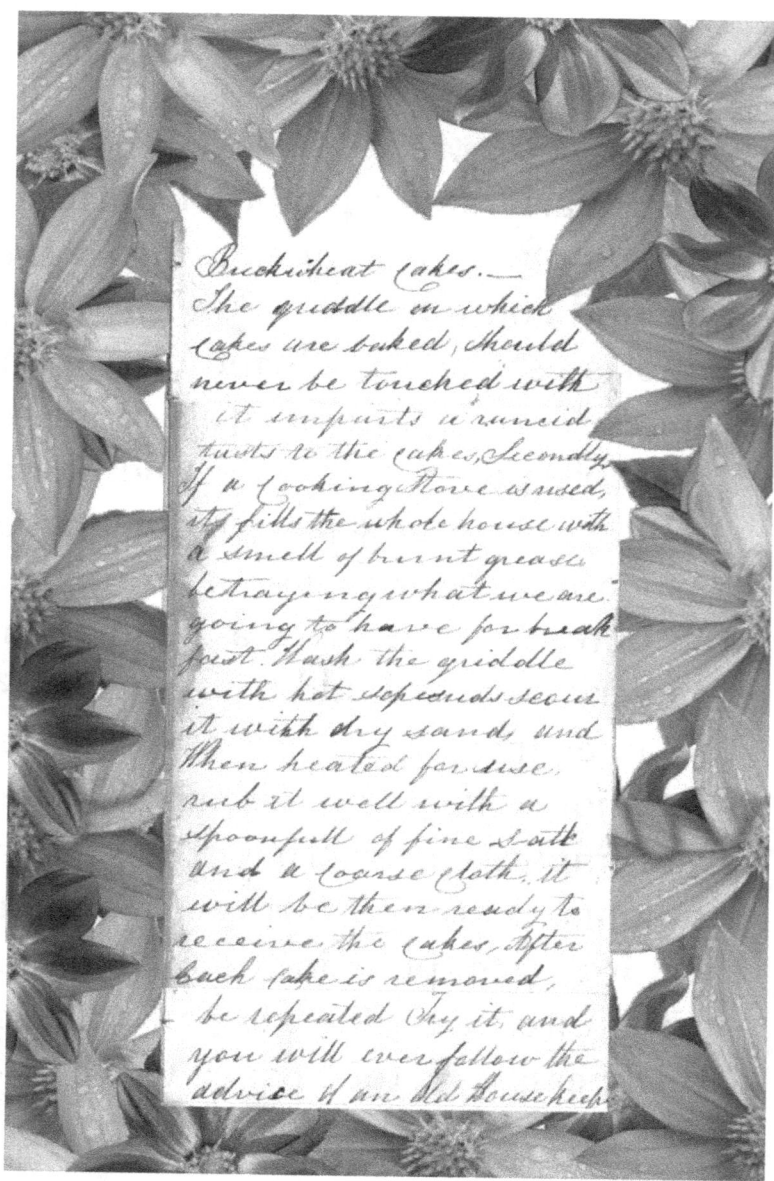

Buckwheat Cakes.—
The griddle on which cakes are baked, should never be touched with [grease?] it imparts a rancid taste to the cakes, Secondly, If a Cooking Stove is used, it fills the whole house with a smell of burnt grease betraying what we are going to have for breakfast. Wash the griddle with hot sopsuds scour it with dry sand, and when heated for use rub it well with a spoonfull of fine Salt and a coarse cloth. it will be then ready to receive the cakes, After each cake is removed, [this must?] be repeated Try it, and you will ever follow the advice of an old housekeeper.

Buckwheat Cakes

The griddle, on which cakes are baked, should never be touched with grease. Firstly, because it imprints a rancid taste to the cakes. Secondly if a cooking stove is used, it fills the whole house with a smell of burnt grease betraying what we are going to have for breakfast. Wash the griddle with soft soap suds, scour it with dry sand, and when heated for use rub it well with a spoonful of fine salt and a course cloth, it will be then ready to receive the cakes. After each cake is removed the salt rubbing must be repeated Try it, and you will ever follow the advice of an Old Housekeeper.

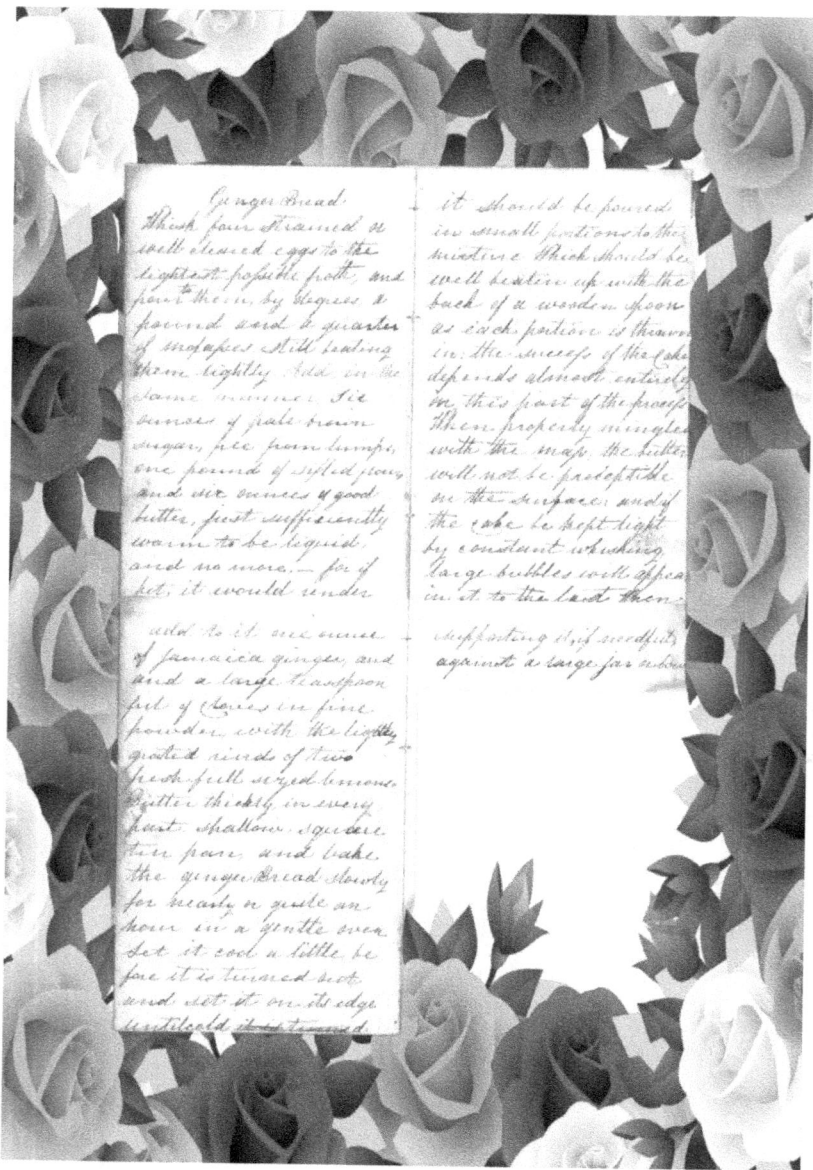

Ginger Bread

Whisk four strained or well cleaned eggs to the lightest possible froth, and pour to them, by degrees, a pound and a quarter of molasses, still beating them lightly. Add in the same manner six ounces of pale brown sugar, free from lumps, one pound of sifted flour, and six ounces of good butter, just sufficiently warm to be liquid, and no more — for if hot, it would render

add to it one ounce of Jamaica ginger, and a large teaspoonful of cloves in fine powder, with the lightly grated rinds of two fresh full sized lemons. Butter thickly in every part shallow square tin pans, and bake the ginger bread slowly for nearly or quite an hour in a gentle oven. Set it cool a little before it is turned out, and set it on its edge until cold it was turned

it should be poured in small portions to the mixture which should be well beaten up with the back of a wooden spoon as each portion is thrown in. The success of the cake depends almost entirely on this part of the process. When properly mingled with the syrup, the butter will not be perceptible on the surface, and if the cake be kept light by constant whisking, large bubbles will appear in it to the last then

supporting it if needful against a large jar when

Ginger Bread

Whisk four strained or well-cleared eggs to the lightest possible froth, and pour to them by degrees a pound and a quarter of Molasses, still beating them lightly add in the same manner, six ounces of pale brown sugar free from lumps, one pound of sifted flour, and six ounces of good butter just sufficiently warm to be liquid no more for if hot it would render the cake heavy. It should be poured in small portions to the mixture, which should be well beaten up with the back of a wooden spoon as each portion is thrown in; the success of the cakes depends almost entirely on this part of the process. when properly mingled with the mass, the butter will not be perceptible

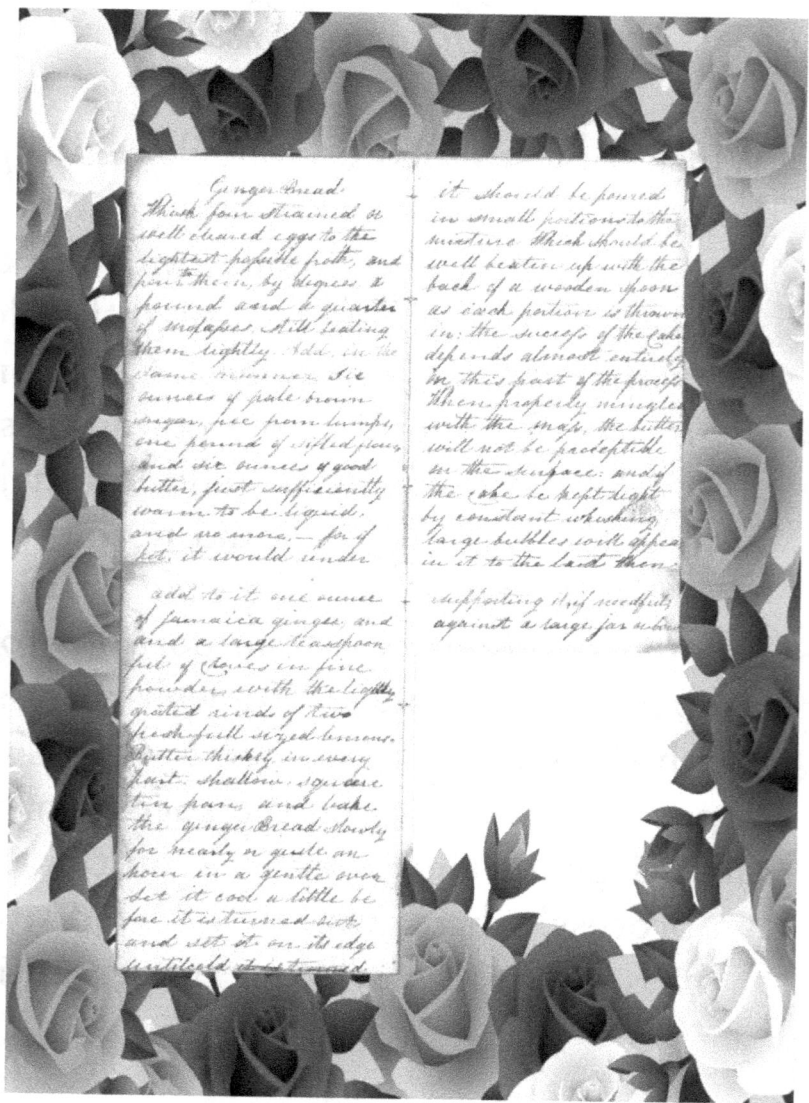

Ginger Bread.

Whisk four strained or well cleared eggs to the lightest possible froth, and pour them, by degrees a pound and a quarter of molasses. Still beating them lightly. Add, in the same manner six ounces of pale brown sugar, free from lumps, one pound of sifted flour, and six ounces of good butter, just sufficiently warm to be liquid, and no more,— for if hot, it would render

add to it one ounce of Jamaica ginger, and and a large teaspoonful of cloves in fine powder, with the lightly grated rinds of two fresh full sized lemons. Butter thickly in every part, shallow, square tin pans, and bake the ginger bread slowly for nearly or quite an hour in a gentle oven. Set it cool a little before it is turned out, and set it on its edge until cold

it should be poured in small portions to the mixture which should be well beaten up with the back of a wooden spoon as each portion is thrown in: the success of the cake depends almost entirely on this part of the process. When properly mingled with the mass, the butter will not be perceptible on the surface: and if the cake be kept light by constant whisking, large bubbles will appear in it to the last then

supporting itself modestly against a large jar when

Ginger Bread (continued)

on the surface; and if the cake be kept light constant whisking, large bubbles will appear in it to the last when it is so far ready Add to it one ounce of Jamaica Ginger and a large teaspoonful of cloves in fine powder, with the lightly grated rinds of two fresh full sized lemons. Butter thickly in every part, shallow square tin pan, and bake the ginger bread slowly for nearly or quite an hour in a gentle oven. Set it cool a little before it is turned out, and set it on its edge until cold, setting it, if needful, against a large jar or bowl.

Lemon Cheese Cakes

Take two large lemons and rub the rind with one pound of loaf sugar so that all the yellow part is removed. Place the sugar in a basin, squeeze the juice of the lemons over, then add the yolks of six eggs, and beat it well up, and put it by in a jar for use. It will keep for years. Any flavor, such as vanilla or cinnamon, may be added, if liked, when required for use. Having made the paste and lined the tins, mix one tablespoonful of the mixture with a teacupful of good milk, and place a little in each tartlet.

Lemon Cheese Cakes

Take two large lemons, and rub the rind with 1 pound of loaf sugar so that all the yellow part is removed: place the sugar in a basin squeeze the juice of the lemons over, then add the yolks of six eggs, and beat it well up, and put it by in a jar for use it will keep for years. Any flavor such as vanilla or Cinnamon may be added if liked, when required for use. Having made the paste, and lined the tins mix one teaspoonful of the mixture with a teacupful of milk, and place a little in each tartlet.

Scotch Short Cake

Mrs Dods receipt.

To the forth of a peck of flour take six ounces of sifted sugar, and of candied orange peel, citron, and blanched almonds two ounces each, cut in rather large pieces and mix with the flour. Rub down in the flour a pound of butter in very small bits, and melt this work up the flour, the less kneading it gets the more short and crisp the cake will be. Roll out the pate into a large well shaped cake, about an inch and a half thick, or divide this, pinch the cakes neatly at the edges, and mark them on the top with an instrument made for the purpose, or with a fork. Strew caraway comfits on the top and a few strips of citron. Bake on paper. Plainer short bread may be made by using less butter. The whole of the butter may be melted, which makes the process easier.

Scotch Short Cake

To the forth of a peck of flour take six ounces of sugar and of candied orange, peels of citron, and blanched almonds two ounces each, cut in rather larger pieces, and mix with the flour. Rub down in the flour a pound of butter in very small bits and melt this, work up the flour the less kneading it gets the more short and crisp the cake will be. Roll out the pate into a large well shaped oval cake about an inch and a half thick and divide this, pinch the cakes neatly at the edges, and mark them on the top with an instrument made for that purpose, or with a fork. Strew Caraway Comfits on the top and a few strips of citron, Bake on paper rubbed with flour. Plainer shortbread may be made by using less butter, the whole of the butter may be melted which makes the process easier.

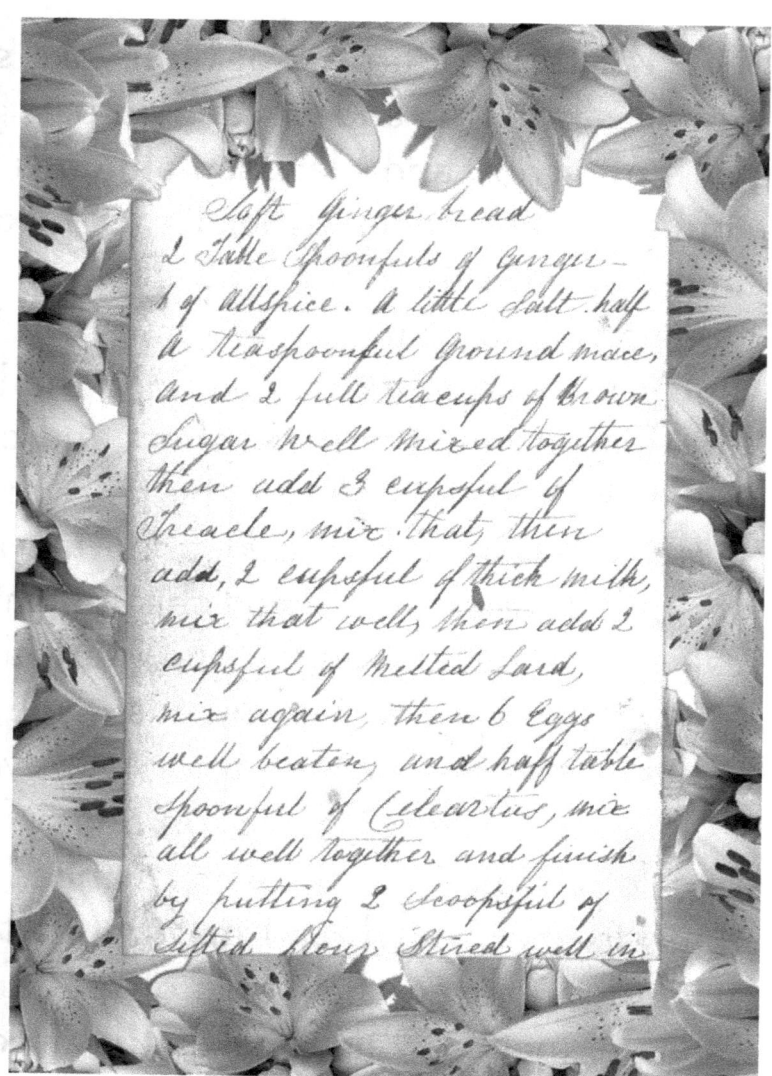

Soft Ginger bread
2 Table Spoonfuls of Ginger —
1 of Allspice. A little Salt, half
a teaspoonful Ground mace,
and 2 full teacups of brown
Sugar well mixed together
then add 3 cupsful of
Treacle, mix that, then
add, 2 cupsful of thick milk,
mix that well, then add 2
cupsful of Melted Lard,
mix again, then 6 Eggs
well beaten, and half table
Spoonful of Celeartus, mix
all well together and finish
by putting 2 Scoopsful of
Sifted flour Stired well in.

Soft Ginger Bread

2 tablespoonfuls of ginger 1 of all spice. A little salt, half a teaspoonful ground mace, and 2 full teacups of brown sugar well mixed together, then add three cupsful of treacle, mix that, then add 2 cupsful of thick milk, mix that well, then add 2 cupfuls of melted lard mix again, then 6 eggs well beaten, and half a tablespoonful of celeritus, mix all well together and finish by putting 2 scoopsful of sifted flour, stirred well in, Bake in a moderate oven.

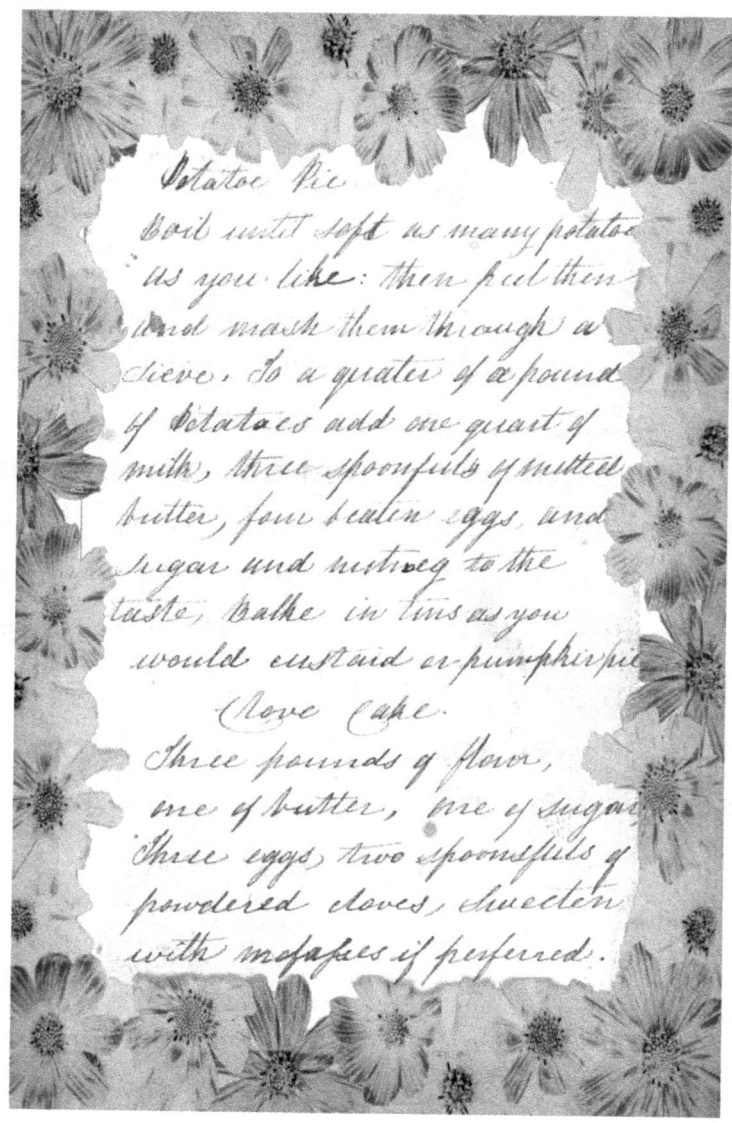

Potatoe Pie

Boil until soft as many potatoes as you like: then peel them and mash them through a sieve. To a quarter of a pound of potatoes add one quart of milk, three spoonfuls of melted butter, four beaten eggs, and sugar and nutmeg to the taste, bake in tins as you would custard or pumpkin pie

Clove Cake

Three pounds of flour, one of butter, one of sugar, three eggs, two spoonsfuls of powdered cloves, sweeten with molasses if preferred.

Potato Pie

Boil until soft as many potatoes as you like: then peel them and mash them through a sieve. To a quarter of a pound of potatoes add one quart of milk, three spoonfuls of melted butter four beaten eggs, and sugar and nutmeg to the taste, Bake in tins as you would custard or pumpkin pie.

Clove Cake.
Three pounds of flour,
one of butter, one of sugar
three eggs, two spoonsfuls of
powdered cloves, sweeten
with molasses if preferred.

Carolina Cake
Two coffee cups sugar
of flour, 1 of sweet cream
whites of 5 eggs, 2 table
spoonsful butter, 1 teaspoon

Clove Cake

Three pounds of flour, 1 of butter, one of sugar, 3 eggs, two spoonfuls of powdered cloves, sweeten with molasses if preferred..

Carolina Cake

Two coffee cups of sugar, 3 of flour, 1 of sweet cream, whites of 5 eggs, 2 tablespoons of butter, 1 teaspoon of extract of lemon, 1 teaspoon of extract of tarter, ½ a teaspoon of soda or 3 eggs is as good.

Scotch Loaf:
Sift a pound of fine sugar,
then whisk the ~~same~~ 9 eggs
and beat both together for
twenty minutes, season
with lemon and grated
Cinnamon. Stir in very
smoothly three quarters of
a pound of sifted flour.
This is a very light cake
and will bake quickly,
Before baking strew over
it pounded sugar. —

Scotch Loaf

Sift a pound of fine sugar, then whisk the 9 eggs and beat both together for twenty minutes. Season with lemon and grated cinnamon, stir in very smoothly three quarters of a pound of sifted flour. This is a very light cake and will bake quickly. Before baking strew over it pounded sugar.

Washington Cake

One pound and three quarters of flour, one pound and a half of sugar, three quarters of a pound of butter, four eggs, half a pint of sour milk, one teaspoonful of saleratus, dissolved in a little hot water.

Beat the sugar and butter together, add the milk and beaten eggs, then put in the dissolved saleratus, and gradually stir in the flour with a wineglass of brandy or wine, and a small nutmeg grated; beat them well together. Make it in two round cakes, or bake it in square tin pans, in a quick oven, allow fifteen minutes if half an inch deep, thirty minutes if an inch deep, and forty five if an inch and a

Washington Cake

1 pound and three quarters of flour, one pound and a half of sugar, three quarters of a pound of butter, four eggs, half a pint of sour milk, 1 teaspoonful of saleratus dissolved in a little hot water.

Beat the sugar and butter together add the milk and beaten egg, then put in the dissolved saleratus, and gradually stir in the flour with a wineglass of brandy or wine, and a small nutmeg grated; beat them well together. Make it in two round cakes ,or bake it in square tin pans, in a quick oven, allow fifteen minutes if half inch deep, thirty minutes if an inch deep and forty if an inch and a half.

College Puddings.

Beat four eggs yolks and whites together, in a quart of flour, two Spoonfuls of milk, half a nutmeg, a little gingar; and three ounces of pounded sugar, Beat into a smooth batter; then add six ounces of suet, chopped fine, six ounces of Currents, well washed and picked, mix all well together, A glass of brandy or white wine will improve it Bake in an oven in patty pans, twenty minutes

College Pudding

Beat four egg yolks and whites together in a quart basin, with two ounces of flour, two spoonfuls of milk, half a nutmeg, a little ginger, and three ounces of pounded sugar.
Beat into a smooth batter, then add six ounces of suet, chopped fine, six ounces of currents, well washed and picked, mix all well together, A glass of brandy or white wine will improve it. Bake in an oven in pally pans twenty minutes.

Palo-alto Cakes.

Beat half a pound of butter to a cream, with half a pound fine white sugar, put to it five well beaten eggs, a tablespoonful of rose water, the same of brandy, half a nut=meg grated, and half a pound of sifted flour, beat it together until very light; line square tin pans with paper, rubbed over with a bit of sponge dipped in melted butter, put in the mixture half an inch deep, and bake in a moderate oven; when done, take it from the oven, turn the pans upside down, and set the cakes upon; when cold, take off the paper, cut it in small fancy shapes; put a little red jelly in the center of each piece, and with a small syringe, put a border of icing around it.

Palo Alto Cakes

Beat half a pound of butter to a cream, with half a pound of sugar, put to it five well beaten eggs, a tablespoon of rose water, the same of brandy, half a nutmeg grated, and half a pound of sifted flour, beat it together until very light, line square tin pans with paper rubbed over with a bit of sponge dipped in melted butter, put in the mixture an half an inch deep, and bake in a moderate oven, when done, take it from the pans, turn them upside down and set the cakes upon, when cold take off the paper, cut it into small fancy shapes, put a little jelly in the center of each piece, and with a small syringe put a border of icing around it.

Yellow Lady Cake
A new way to make it

Take a pound of fine white sugar with half a pound of butter beaten to a cream, the yolks of eight eggs beaten smooth and thick, one cup of sweet milk, a small teaspoonful of powdered saleratus, salts or saleratus dissolved in a little hot water, half a nutmeg grated, a teaspoonful of lemon extract or orange flower water, and as much sifted wheat flour as will make it as thick as pound cake batter, beat it until it is light and creamy, then having taken the skins from, and beaten to a paste quarter of a pound of shelled almonds, stir them into the cake, beat buttered tin pans with white paper, put in the mixture an inch deep, and bake half an hour in a quick oven or forty minutes in a moderate oven. This is a delicious cake, never before given in any book, being the result of an experiment of the author of this book.

Lady Cake is usually made with the yolks of eggs, as Savoy cake (two yolks for one egg) with the addition of pounded almonds. See it as directed for composition of cake, whites a little

Yellow Lady Cake
A new way to make it

Take a pound of fine white sugar with half a pound of butter beaten to a cream the yolks of eight eggs beaten smooth and thick, one cup of sweet milk, a small teaspoonful of powdered volatile salts or saleacitus, dissolved in a little hot water, half a nutmeg grated, a teaspoonful of lemon extract or orange flower water, and as much sifted flour as will make it as thick as pound cake batter, beat it until it is light and creamy, then having taken the skins from, and beaten to a paste quarter of a pound of shelled almonds, stir them in to the cake beat them in it, line buttered tin pans with white paper, put in the mixture an inch deep, and bake half an hour in a quick oven or forty minutes in a moderate oven.

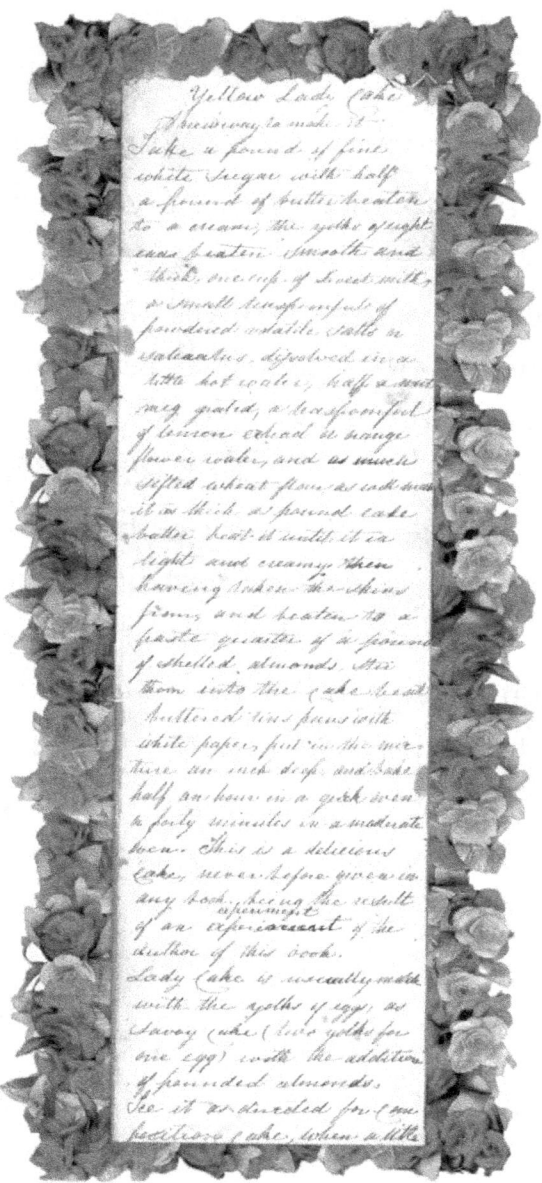

Yellow Lady Cake
Previous way to make it —
Take a pound of fine
white sugar with half
a pound of butter beaten
to a cream; the yolks of eight
eggs beaten smooth and
thick, one cup of sweet milk,
a small teaspoonful of
powdered volatile salts or
saleratus dissolved in a
little hot water, half a nutmeg grated, a teaspoonful
of lemon extract or orange
flower water, and as much
sifted wheat flour as will make
it as thick as pound cake
batter, beat it until it is
light and creamy, then
having taken the whites
firm, and beaten to a
paste, quarter of a pound
of shelled almonds. Stir
them into the cake. Line
buttered tin pans with
white paper, put in the mixture an inch deep, and bake
half an hour in a quick oven
or forty minutes in a moderate
oven. This is a delicious
cake, never before given in
any book, being the result
of an experiment of the
author of this book.
Lady Cake is usually made
with the yolks of eggs, as
Savoy cake (two yolks for
one egg) with the addition
of pounded almonds.
See it as directed for composition cake, when a little

Yellow Lady Cake (continued)

This is a delicious Cake never before given in any book, being the result of an experiment of the author of this book. Lady cake is usually made, as Savoy Cake (two yolks for one egg) with the addition of pounded almonds, Ice it as directed for composition cake, when a little dry mark it with knife.

White Lady Cake.
Beat the whites of eight eggs
to a stiff froth, add gradually
a pound of white sugar finely
ground, beat quarter of a pound
of butter to a cream, add a
teacup of sweet milk with a
small teaspoonful of powdered
volatile salts or Saleratus
dissolved in it, put the eggs
to butters and milk, add as
much sifted wheat flour as
will make it as thick as
pound cake mixture, and a

and beaten to a paste with
a little white of egg; beat the
whole together until light and
white; line a square tin pan
with buttered paper, put
in the mixture an inch deep
and one & half an hour
in a quick oven. When
done take it from the
pans when cold take
the papers off, turn it
upside down on the
bottom of the pan and
ice the side which was
down; when the icing
is nearly hard mark it
off in slices the width of a

One Two Three four Cake.
One cup of butter, two cups
of sugar, three cups of flour
and four eggs. Work the sugar
and butter together, put it
to the eggs well beaten
then mix in the flour
add grated nutmeg, flour
the Cake board or table,
and roll the cake to rath-
more than a quarter of an
inch thick. Prick each
with a fork, and bake
fifteen minutes in a
quick oven

White Lady Cake

Beat the whites of eight eggs to a white froth, and add gradually a pound of white sugar finely ground, beat a quarter of a pound of butter, to a cream, add a teacup of sweet milk with a small teaspoonful of powdered volatile salts or slaeratus dissolved in it, put the eggs to butter and milk add as much sifted wheat flower as will make it as thick as pound cake mixture, and a teaspoonful of orange flower water or lemon extract, then add a quarter of a pound of shelled almonds blanched and beaten to a paste with a little white of egg: beat the whole together until light and white, line a square tin pan with buttered paper put in the mixture an inch deep and bake half an hour in a quick oven.

White Lady Cake —
Beat the whites of eight eggs
to a stiff froth, add gradually
a pound of white sugar finely
pounded, beat quarter of a pound
of Butter to a cream, add a
teacup of sweet milk with a
small teaspoonful of pulverized
volatile salts or saleratus
dissolved in it, put the eggs
to butter and milk, add as
much sifted wheat flour as
well make it as thick as
pound Cake mixture, and a —

and beat in to a paste with
a little white of egg, beat the
whole together until light and
white, line a square tin pan
with buttered paper, put
in the mixture an inch deep
and one & half an hour
in a quick oven, when
done take it from the
pan, when cold take
the paper off, turn it
upside down on the
bottom of the pan and
ice the side which was
down, when the icing
is nearly hard mark
it in slices the width of a

One two three four Cake —
One cup of butter Two cups
of sugar, three cups of flour
and five eggs, Stir the sugar
and butter together, put it
to the eggs well beaten
then mix in the flour
add grated nutmeg, flour
the Cake board or table
and roll the Cake to rather
more than a quarter of an
inch thick, stick each
with a fork, and bake
fifteen minutes in a
quick oven —

White Lady Cake (continued)

When done take it from the pans, when cold take the paper off turn upside down on the bottom of the pan and ice the side which was down, When the icing is nearly hard mark it in pieces the width of a finger and two and a half inches long .

Lemon Pudding —
Beat half a pound of
fresh butter beaten to a
cream with half a pound
of white sugar, powdered
fine, then add to it eight
well beaten, and a large
fresh lemon grated with
the skin, stire it well
together, line a dish with
puff paste fill with the
pudding and bake in a
quick oven for nearly an (hour)

Lemon Pudding

Beat half a pound of fresh butter beaten to a cream with half a pound of white sugar powdered fine, then add to it eight well beaten eggs, and a large lemon grated with the skin, stir it well together, line a dish with puff paste fill it with the pudding and bake in a quick oven for nearly an hour.

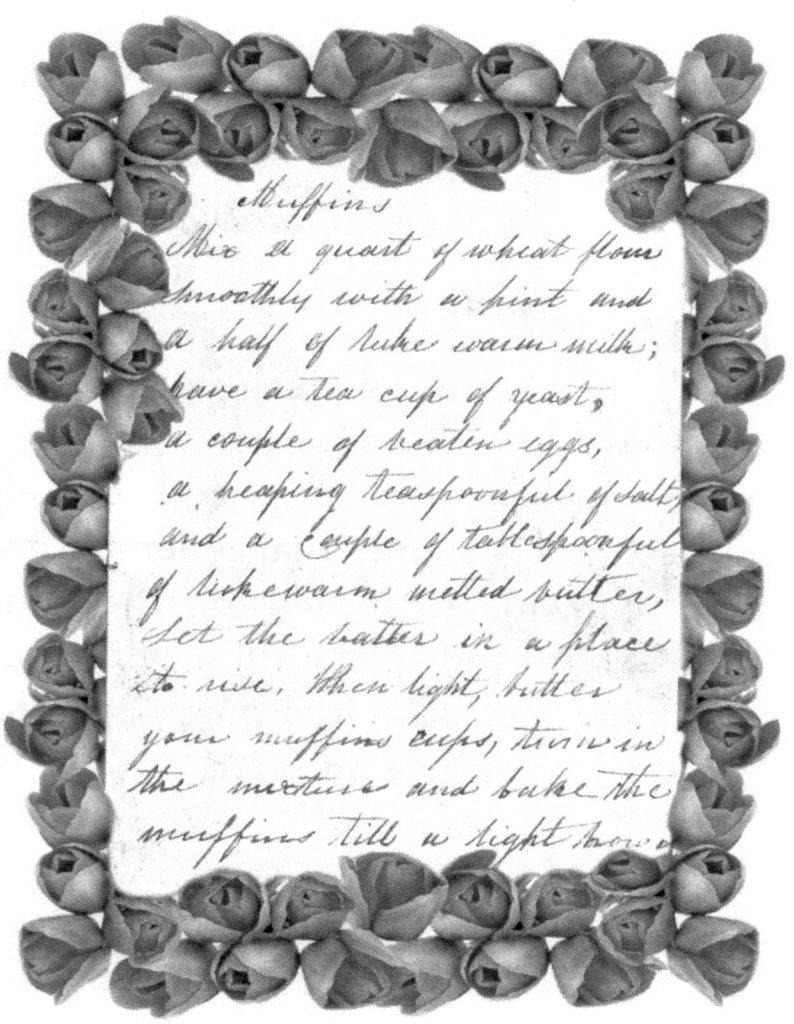

Muffins

Mix a quart of wheat flour smoothly with a pint and a half of luke warm milk; have a tea cup of yeast, a couple of beaten eggs, a heaping teaspoonful of salt, and a couple of tablespoonful of lukewarm melted butter, set the batter in a place to rise. When light, butter your muffins cups, turn in the mixture and bake the muffins till a light brown

Muffins

Mix a quart of wheat flour smoothly with a a pint a half of luke warm milk; have a teacup of yeast, a couple of beaten eggs a heaping teaspoonful of salt and a couple of tablespoonfuls of lukewarm melted butter. Set the batter in a warm place to rise, then light, butter your muffin cups, turn in the mixture, and bake the muffins till a light brown.

To Make Prime Vinegar

A correspondent of the Ohio Cultivator vouches for the merit of the following recipe for making vinegar. Take and mix one quart of Molasses, three gallons of rain water, and pint of yeast. Let it ferment and you will will have the best vinegar.

    Ohio Cultivator

To Make Primo Vinegar

A Correspondent of the Ohio Cultivator vouches for the merit of the following recipe for making vinegar
Take and mix 1 quart of molasses, three gallons of rain water, and pint of yeast
Let it ferment and you will have the best vinegar.

Ohio Cultivator

Sponge Cake — Take the weight of the eggs in sugar, half their their weight in flour, well sifted. To twelve eggs add the grated grated rind of juice of two. Beat the eggs carefully, Whites and yolks separately, before they are used. Stir the materials throughly togeather, and bake in a quick oven

Sponge Cake

Take the weight of the eggs in sugar, half their weight in flour, well sifted to twelve eggs add the grated rind of three lemons, and the juice of two, beat the eggs carefully, whites and yolks seperately before they are used. Stir the materials together, and bake in a quick oven.

Cup Cake

Mix together five cups of flour, three cups of sugar, one cup of butter, one cup of milk, three eggs well beaten, one wine glass of wine, one of brandy and a little cinnamon.

To Make A Corn Cake worth eating

Take the whites of eight eggs, ½ lb Corn Starch, ½ lb Flour, ½ lb Butter, ½ lb Sugar, one Tea-Spoonful Cream a Tartar, half teaspoonful of Soda, flavor with Almond to the taste.

Cup cake

Mix together five cups of flour three cups of sugar, one cup of butter, one cup of milk, three eggs, well beaten, one wine glass of wine one of brandy and a little cinnamon.

To make a corn cake worth eating

Take the whites of eight eggs ¼ lbs corn starch ¼ lbs of flour ¼ pound of butter, 1/2 pound of sugar 1 teaspoonful cream of tarter, half teaspoonful of soda, flavor with almond as to the taste.

A Recipe for Making Hot
    Cross Buns:—
Rub four ounces of butter
into two pounds of sugar, an
ounce and a half of ground
Allspice, cinnamon, and mace
mixed. Put a spoonful or
two of cream into a cup of
as will make the above into a
good paste. Set it before the fire
to rise. The buns will bake
quickly on tins. When half baked
press the form of a cross with
a tin mould in the centre—
                London Recipe.

A Recipe for Making Hot Cross Buns

Rub four ounces of sugar into two pounds of sugar, an ounce and a half of ground allspice, cinnamon, and mace mixed. Put a spoonful or two of cream into a cup of yeast, and as much milk as will make the above into a good paste. Set it before the fire to rise. The buns will bake quickly on tins. When half baked press the form of a cross with a tin mould in the center.

London Recipe.

Artificial Oysters.

Take young green corn, grate it in a dish. To one pint of this add one egg well beaten, a small tea cup butter, some salt and pepper, and mix them well together. A tablespoonful of the batter will make the size of an oyster. Fry them a light brown, and when done butter them. Cream, if it can be procured, is better than batter than butter.

Artificial Oysters

Take young green corn, grate it in a dish to one pint of this add one egg well beaten, a small tea cup of butter, some salt and pepper and mix them well together. A tablespoon of the batter will make the size of the oyster by then a light brown and when done butter them, Cream, if it can be procured is better them, is better than butter.

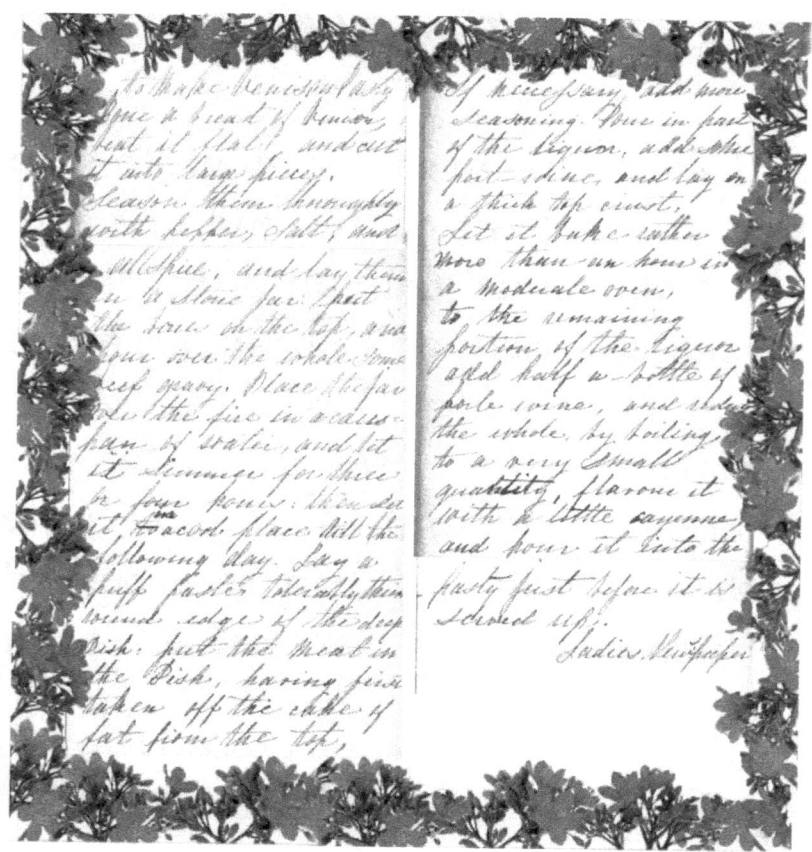

To make Venison Pasty.
Take a breast of venison, beat it flat, and cut it into large pieces. Season them thoroughly with pepper, salt, and allspice, and lay them in a stone jar. Put the bones on the top, and pour over the whole some beef gravy. Place the jar on the fire in a cassepan of water, and let it simmer for three or four hours; then set it in a cool place till the following day. Lay a puff paste tolerably thick round edge of the deep dish; put the meat in the dish, having first taken off the cake of fat from the top, if necessary add more seasoning. Pour in part of the liquor, add some port-wine, and lay on a thick top crust. Let it bake rather more than an hour in a moderate oven. To the remaining portion of the liquor add half a bottle of port wine, and reduce the whole by boiling to a very small quantity; flavour it with a little cayenne, and pour it into the pasty just before it is served up.

Ladies Newspaper

To Make a Venison Pasty

Bone a breast of venison, beat it flat and cut it into large pieces, Season them thoroughly with pepper salt and allspice, and lay them in a stone jar: pact the bones over the top, and pour over the whole some beef gravy. Place the jar over the fire in a caisse pan of water, and let simmer for three of four hours then let it aside a cool place until the following day. Lay a puff pasty tolerably thick around the edge of the deep dish: put the meat in the dish, having first taken of the cake of fat from the top. If necessary add more seasoning.. Pour in part of the liquor, add some port wine, and lay on a thick crust, Let it bake rather more than an hour in a moderate oven. To the remaining portion of the liquor add half a bottle of port wine and reduce the whole by, by boiling it to a very small quantity, flavor it with a little cayenne and pour it into the pasty just before it is served up.

Ladies newspaper

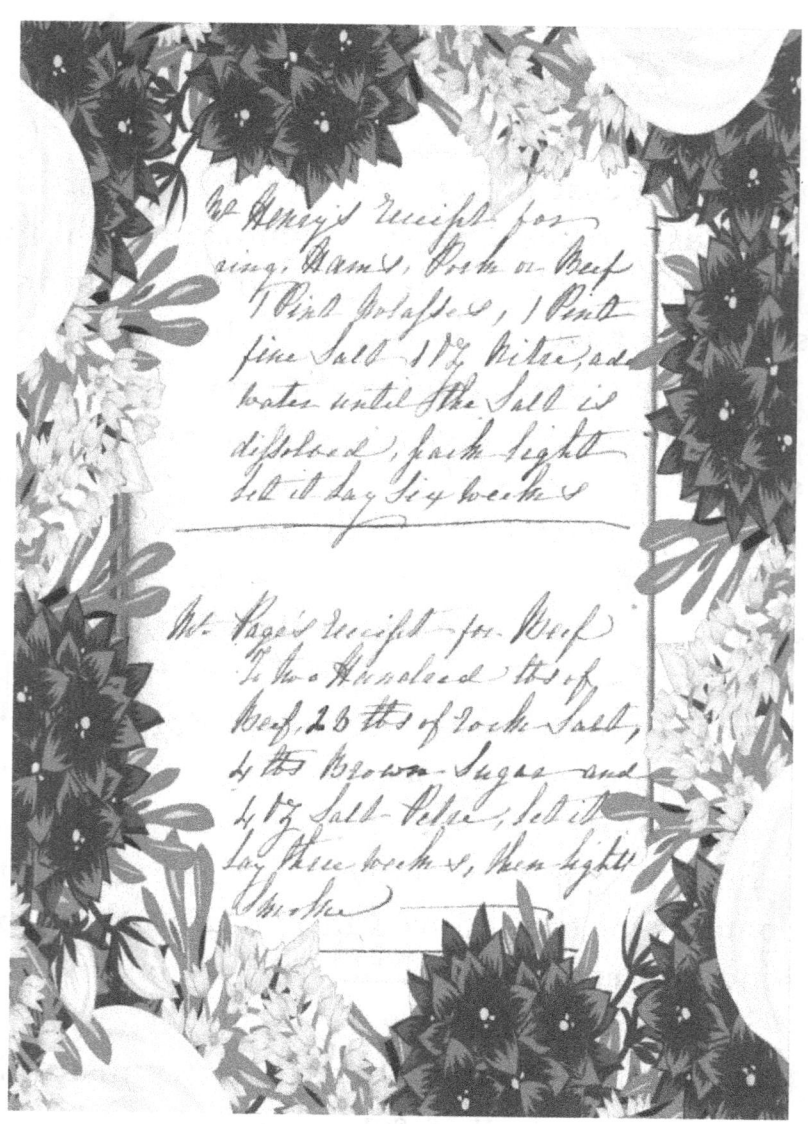

Mr Henry's receipt for
ing Hams, Pork or Beef
1 Pint Molasses, 1 Pint
fine Salt 1 oz Nitre, add
water until the Salt is
dissolved, pack tight
let it lay Six weeks

Mr Page's receipt for Beef
To two Hundred lbs of
Beef, 2 lbs of Rock Salt,
4 lbs Brown Sugar and
4 oz Salt Petre, let it
lay three weeks, then light
Smoke

Mr. Henry's Recipe for Curing Ham, Pork, or Beef

1 Pint of molasses, 1 Pint of fine salt 1 oz of nitre, add water until the salt is dissolved, pack light let lay six weeks.

Mr. Page's Recipe for Beef

To two hundred pounds of beef, 23 lbs of rock salt, 4 lbs of brown sugar, and 4 oz of salt peter, let it lay for three weeks and then lightly smoke.

To make Cheesecakes

Put a Spoonful of rennet into a quart of Milk, when turned; drain the curd the Whey, then rub the following ingredients well together, A ¼ lb Butter, A ¼ lb Sugar, Some nutmeg, two biscuits grated, the yolks of four Eggs, the white of one, half oz of Almonds "half bitter, half Sweet" well beaten in A Mortar, and 4 oz of Currents; lastly, mix the curd with the above having first gently bruised it

To make Cheesecake

Put a spoonful of rennet into a quart of milk, when turned drain the curd the whey, then rub the following ingredients well together A ¼ pound of butter, a ¼ pound of sugar, Some nutmeg, two biscuits grated, the yolks of four eggs, the white of one, 1/2 oz of almonds "half bitter, half sweet" well beaten in a mortar and 4 oz of currants; mix the curd with the above, having first gently brushed it.

A recipe for Gingerbread
Rub one pound of butter
well into three pounds
of flour; then add one
pound of powdered sugar
one pound of treacle, two
ounces of ground ginger,
and one nutmeg grated.
Warm a quarter of a pint
of cream and mix all
together. Make it into a
stiff paste and bake it in
a slow oven. Carraways
and sweetmeats may
be added if desired

A Recipe for Gingerbread

Rub one pound of butter into three pounds of flour: the add 1 pound of powdered sugar one pound of treacle, two ounces of ground ginger, and one nutmeg grated. Warm a quarter of a pint of cream, and milk all together, make it into a stiff paste and bake it in a slow oven.
Caraways and sweetmeats may be added if desired.

A very excellent
  Pudding
Stew until very tender
and do three ounces
of whole rice in a pint
and a quarter of milk,
when a little cooled
mix with it three ounces
of beef suet, finely chopped
two ounces and a half of
powdered sugar one ounce
of candied orange and
lemon peel, six ounces
of sultana raisins, and
three large eggs and
strained. Boil the pudding
in a buttered basin
or in a well floured cloth
for two hours and a
quarter, and serve with
a sauce made as follows

Dissolve an ounce and
and a half of lump sugar
in two glasses of white
wine, and stir in the
beaten yolks of three eggs,
then warm them in a
saucepan holding the pan
at a distance over the
fire and stirring it round
By no means allow it to
boil or it will immediately
curdle. Pour the sauce
over the pudding or if
preferred send it to
table in a tureen

A very excellent Pudding

Stew until very tender and dry three ounces of whole rice in a pint and quarter of milk. When a little cooled mix with it three ounces of beef suet, finely chopped two ounces and a half of powdered sugar, one ounce of candied orange and lemon peel, six ounces of sultans raisins, and three large eggs and strained. Boil the pudding in a buttered basin, or in a well floured cloth for two hours and a quarter and serve with a sauce as follows.

Dissolve an ounce and a half of lump sugar in two glasses of white wine and stir in the beaten yolks of three eggs then warm them in a saucepan holding the pan at a distance over the fire and stirring it round By no means allow it to boil or it will immediately curdle. Pour the sauce over the pudding or if preferred send it to the table in a tureen.

Maccaroni is usually served thus. Boil it in milk, or weak veal broth, pretty well flavoured with salt. When tender, put it into a dish without the liquor, mix into it some bits of butter and grated cheese, then over the top grate a little more, and add a little more butter. Set the Dish in to a Dutch oven for a quarter of an hour, but do not let the top become hard.

Maccaroni

Maccaroni is usually served like this. Boil it in Milk or weak veal broth, pretty well flavored with salt. When tender, put it in a dish without the liquid, mix into it some bits of butter and grated cheese then over the top a little more and a little more butter. Set the dish into a Dutch oven for a quarter of an hour, but do not let the top become hard.

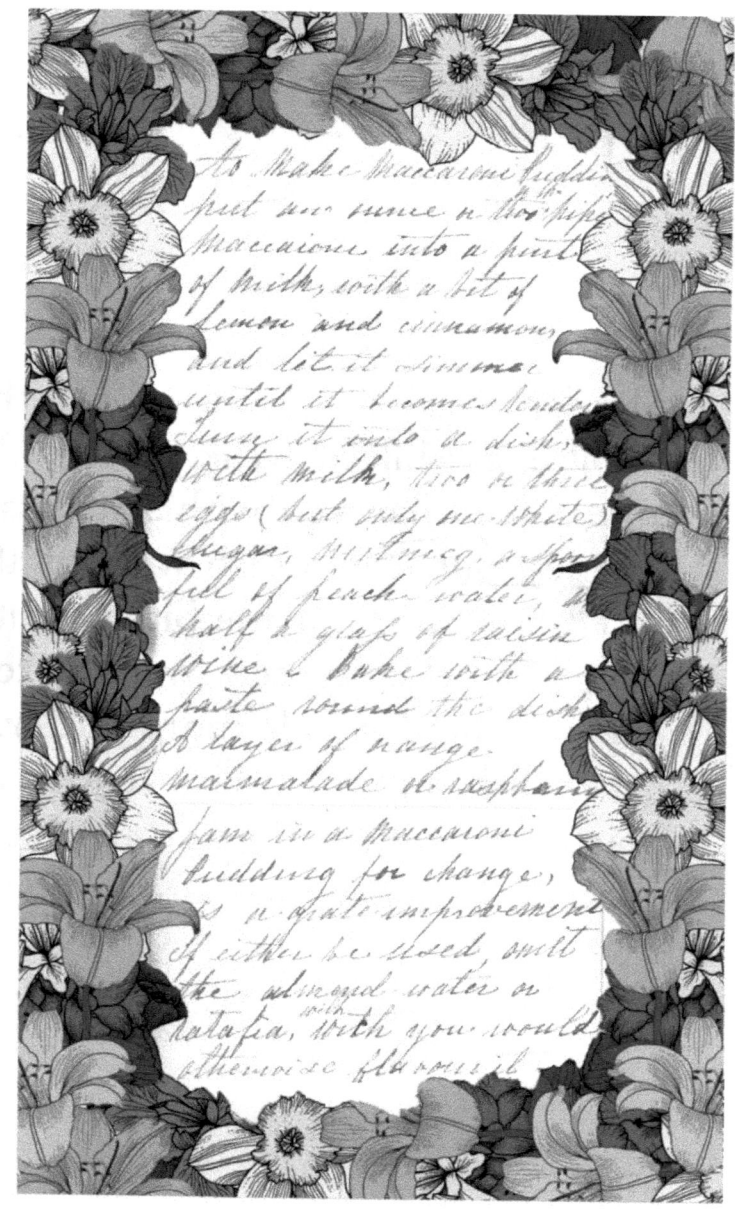

To make Maccaroni pudding put an ounce or thos pipe Maccaroni into a pint of milk, with a bit of lemon and cinnamon, and let it simmer until it becomes tender, turn it into a dish, with milk, two or three eggs (but only one white) sugar, nutmeg, a spoonfull of peach water, & half a glass of raisin wine & bake with a paste round the dish. A layer of orange marmalade or raspberry jam in a maccaroni pudding for change, is a great improvement. If either be used, omit the almond water or ratafia, with you would otherwise flavour it

A Maccaroni Pudding

Take Maccaroni put an ounce or two of the pipe macaroni into a pint of milk with a bit of lemon and cinnamon and let it simmer until it becomes tender Turn it in to dish, with milk, two or three eggs (but only one white) sugar, nutmeg, a spoonful of peach water, a half a glass of raisin wine, bake with a paste round the dish. A layer of orange marmalade or raspberry jam on a macaroni pudding for a change, is a great improvement if either be used omit the almond water or rotated with which you would otherwise flavor it.

Corn Bread,

Mix up with warm water enough to make a thin dough, two quarts of Indian meal; add a teaspoonful of salt, one half pint of molasses, one tablespoonful of dissolved saleratus and one quart of rye meal, with water enough to make it of the proper consistency for a loaf. Bake four hours in the oven is none to much time; how to eat it, When it is cold, and never before cut off some slices and lay them lightly in a pan so that no two shall overlap; put them in the stove oven and shut the door.
eat warm

Corn Bread

Mix up with warm water enough to make a thin dough, two quarts of Indian meal, add a teaspoonful of salt, one half pint of molasses, one tablespoon of dissolved salaeratus and one quart of rye meal, with water to make it the proper consistency for a loaf. Bake 4 hours is none to much. Now, how to eat it. When it is cold, and never before, cut off some slices, lay them lightly in a pan so that no two shall overlap: put them in the stove oven and shut the door.

Let warm.

The French Pot au Feu – a
national soup of France.
Put a Gallon of water in the pot;
put four lbs of the buttock of Beef,
or shin, or five pounds of the
thick part of the leg – three teaspoon
fuls of salt, one of pepper, four
onions, four leeks, cut in pieces
two carrots, and two good
sized turnips, three cloves, —
one burnt onion, or three spoon
fuls of coloring; set it on the
fire; when beginning to scum,
skim it and set the pot on
one side of the fire. Add now
and then a drop of cold water;
it will make it clear. Boil

put into the tureen, and pour
the broth with some of the
vegetables over; serve the
meat separate, and the
remaining vegetables round.

The French Pot au Feu or National soup of France

Put a gallon of Water in the pot, put four lbs of the buttock of beef, or shin, or five pounds of the thick part of the leg, three teaspoonfuls of salt ,one of pepper, four onions, four leeks, cut in pieces, two carrots and two good size turnips, three cloves, one burnt onion, or three spoonfuls of coloring; set it on the fire; when beginning to scum skim it and set the pot on one side of the fire. Add now and then a drop of cold water it will make it clear. Boil and put it into the tureen, and pour the broth with some of the vegetable over; serve the, meat separate, and the remaining vegetables around.

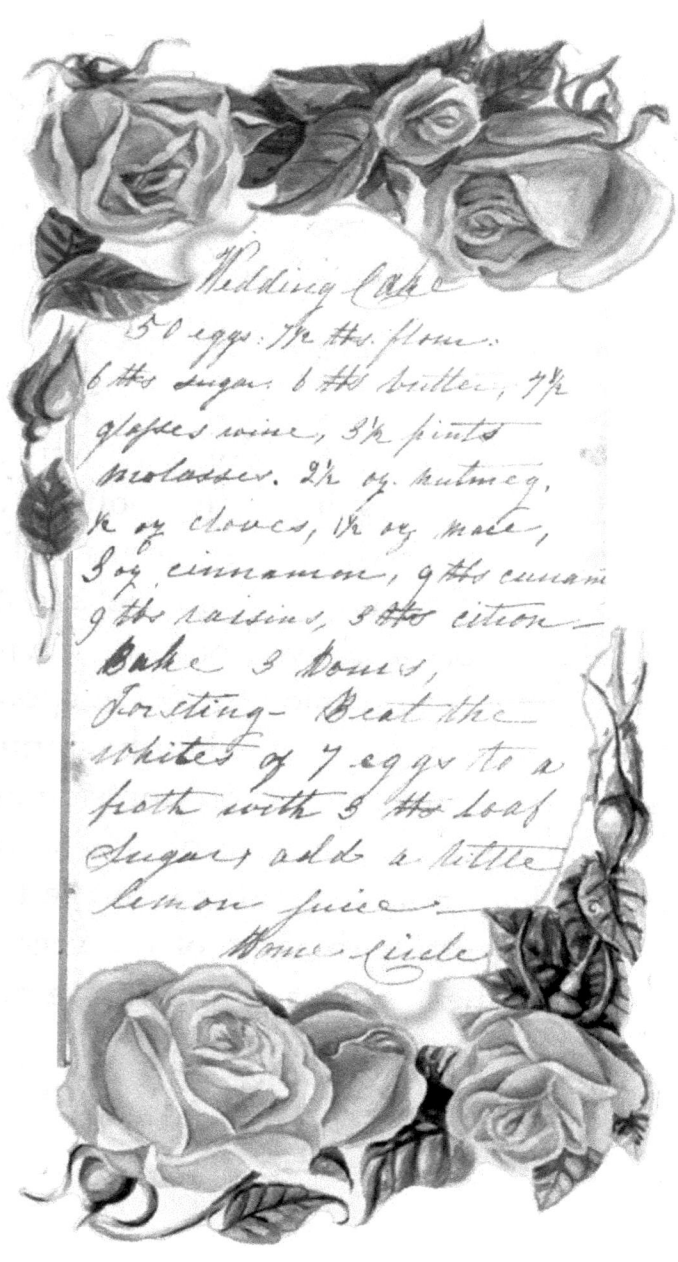

Wedding Cake
50 eggs. 7½ ℔s flour.
6 ℔s sugar, 6 ℔s butter, 7½
glasses wine, 3½ pints
molasses. 2½ oz. nutmeg,
½ oz cloves, ½ oz mace,
3 oz cinnamon, 9 ℔s currants
9 ℔s raisins, 3 ℔s citron
Bake 3 hours.
Frosting— Beat the
whites of 7 eggs to a
froth with 3 ℔ loaf
sugar, add a little
lemon juice.
Home Circle

Wedding Cake

50 eggs, 7 ½ lbs flour 6 lbs of sugar 6 lbs of butter, 7½ glasses of wine, 3½ pints of molasses, 2½ ounces of nutmeg ½ ounce of cloves, 1½ ounce of mace 3oz of cinnamon, 9 lbs of currants, 9lbs of raisins, 3lbs of citron, Bake 3 Hours,
Frosting- Beat the whites of 7 eggs to a froth with 3 pounds of loaf sugar, add a little lemon.

Home Circle

Pork Sausage, of a very
Superior flavor and quality.
To one hundred pounds of
pork, add eight ounces
of Mustard, 8 ounces of
Black pepper, two ounces
of Salt-petre, one pound
of Sugar, and six pounds
of fine Salt.

Pork Sausage of a very Superior Flavor and Quality

To one hundred pounds of pork, add eight ounces of mustard, 8 ounces of black pepper, two ounces of salt-Petri. One pound of sugar, and six pounds of fine salt.

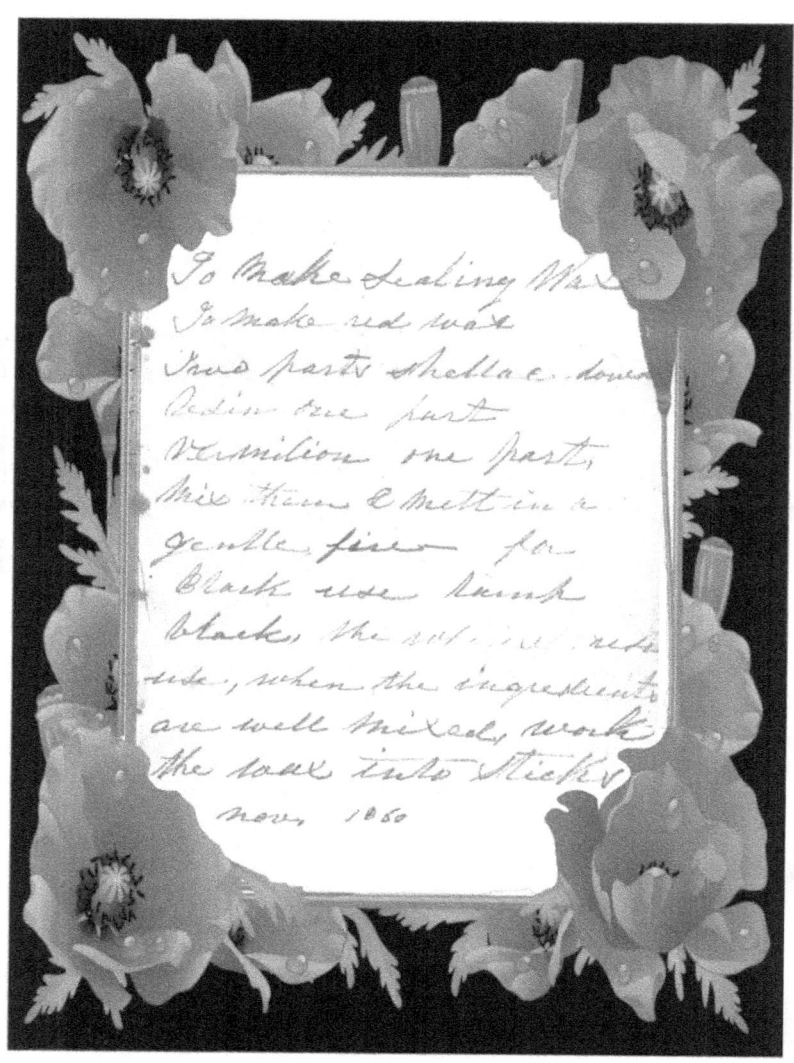

To Make Sealing Wax
To make red wax
Two parts shellac done
resin one part
Vermilion one part,
Mix them & mett in a
gentle fire — for
Black use lamp
black the same as red
use, when the ingredients
are well mixed, work
the same into sticks
nov, 1860

To make Sealing Wax

To make red wax two parts shellac, powdered resin one part, vermillion one part, mix them and melt in a gentle fire, for black use lamp black, the whitest sides use, when the ingredients are well mixed work them into sticks

Nov 1850

Soft Ginger Bread.
Take 5 tea cups of flour
2 cups of molasses, 1 of cream
1 of butter, 1 spoonful of
pearlash, 2 tablespoonfuls
ginger, 1 of allspice.

Portable Lemonade.—
Powdered sugar 2 pounds
Citric acid half an ounce
Essence of Lemon, 1 drachm
mix well. Two to three
teaspoonfuls make a glass
of Lemonade.—

Soft Ginger Bread

Take 5 teacups of flour, 2 teacups of molasses, 1 of cream, 1 of butter 1 teaspoonful of pearlash, 2 tablespoonfuls ginger, 1 of allspice.

Portable Lemonade

Powdered sugar, 2 pounds citric acid, ½ ounce essence of lemon 1 drachm, mix well; two to three teaspoonfuls make a glass of lemonade.

Gâteau de Pommes

Boil together, for a quarter of an hour, a pound of White sugar and half a pint of Water, then add 2 pounds of any finely flavoured apples, which can be boiled to a smooth pulp, add the juice of 1 large lemon. Stew until the mixture is free from lumps, and then boil it quickly, stirring constantly until it forms a very thick and dry marmalade. Before it is quite done, add the finely grated rinds of 2 lemons. When it of the preserving pan visible and dry, press it into moulds of tasteful form, and store it for future use, or if wanted for table serve it plain for dessert, or ornament it with spikes of blanched almonds and pour a custard round it. —

Gateau de Pommes

Boil together for a quarter of an hour a pound of white sugar, and a half pint of water, then add 2 pounds of any finely flavored apples, which can be boiled to a smooth pulp, add the juice of 1 large lemon, stew until the mixture is free from lumps, and then boil it quickly stirring constantly until it forms a very thick and dry marmalade, before it is quite done, add the finely grated rinds of 2 lemons. When it leaves the bottom of the preserving pan visible and dry, press it into moulds of tasteful form, and store it for future use, or if wanted for table serve it plain for dessert, or ornament it with spikes of blanched almonds, and pour a custard around it:

Rice Cup Pudding

Pick and wash, A teacup full of rice, and boil it in a quart of Milk till it is very thick and dry, add to this, whilst it is hot, A pint of new Milk or cream, and two oz. of Butter. When it is sufficiently cool, add three Eggs, well beaten—cups, pour in the Mixture, and bake in a Moderate oven. grate nutmeg over the top, and serve with sweetened cream.

Rice Cup Pudding

Pick and wash a teacup full of rice, and boil it in a quart of milk till it is very thick and dry, add to this whilst it is very hot, a pint of rich milk or cream, and 2 oz of butter, When it is sufficiently cool, add three eggs well beaten, add sugar to taste, butter your cups, pour in the mixture and bake in a moderate oven, Serve with sweetened cream.

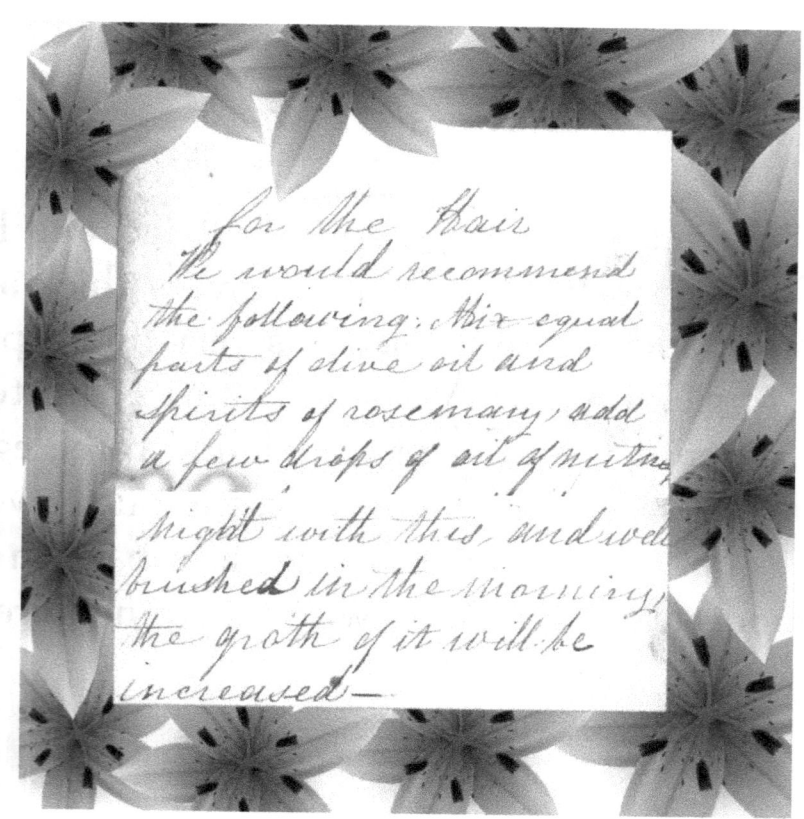

For the Hair

We would recommend the following: Mix equal parts of olive oil and spirits of rosemary, add a few drops of oil of nutmeg, night with this and well brushed in the morning, the growth of it will be increased—

For the Hair

We would recommend the following: mix equal parts of olive oil, and spirits of rosemary, add a few drops of oil of nutmeg. If the hair be scrubbed every night with this, and well brushed in the morning the growth of it will be increased.

Scotch Loaf:
   Sift a pound of fine sugar,
then whisk the ~~same~~ 9 eggs
and beat both together for
twenty minutes, season
with lemon and grated
cinnamon. Stir in very
smoothly three quarters of
a pound of sifted flour.
This is a very light cake
and will bake quickly,
Before baking strew over
   it pounded sugar —

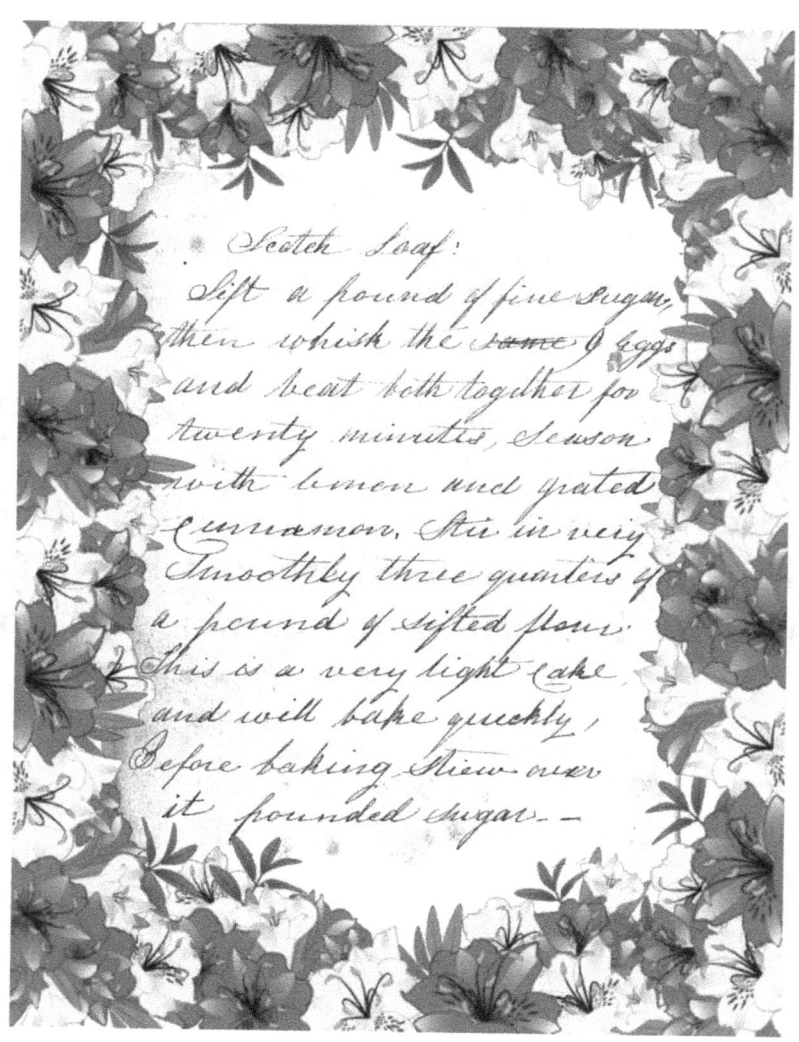

Scotch Loaf

Sift a pound of fine sugar then whisk 9 eggs and beat both together for twenty minutes season with lemon and grated cinnamon, stir in very smoothly three quarters of a pound of sifted flour, This is a very light cake and will bake quickly, before baking strew over it pounded sugar.

Quince Jelly.

Quinces for jelly should not be quite ripe, they should be a fine yellow, rub off the down from them, core them, and cut them small; put them in a preserving kettle, with a teacup of water for each pound, let them stew gently until soft, without mashing, put them in a thin muslin with the liquor, press them very slightly; to each pint of the liquor put a pound of sugar; stir it until it is all dissolved, then set it over the fire and it boil gently, until by cooling some on a plate, you find it a good jelly, then turn it into pots or tumblers, and when cold, secure as directed for jelly.

Quince Jelly

Quinces for jelly should not be quite ripe, they should be a fine yellow, rub off the down from them, core them, and cut them small, put them in a preserving kettle, with a teacup of water for each pound, let them stew gently until soft without mashing, put them in a thin muslin with the liquor, press them very slightly, to each pint of the liquor put a pound of sugar, stir it until it is all dissolved, then set it over the fire and it boil gently, until by cooling some on a plate, you find it a good jelly, then turn it into pots or tumblers, and when cold, secure as directed for jelly.

Scotch Loaf
3 cups of fine sugar
9 eggs. Beat both together
for twenty minutes,
Season with lemon and
ground cinnamon,
Stir in very smoothly
3 cups of flour.
Before baking strew over
it white sugar.
            Elizabeth Cobham

Scotch Loaf

3 cups of fine sugar, 9 eggs. Beat both together for twenty minutes, season with lemon and ground cinnamon stir in very smoothly 3 cups of flour. Before baking strew over it white sugar

Elizabeth Cobham

To cure Hams
Take of rock Salt 9 ℔s,
Salt Petre 6 oz, Molases
3 Pints, for 1 hundred
℔s of Meat, this is a
Simple, but excelent
receipt

To Cure Hams

Take of rock salt 9 lbs, of salt petre 6 oz, molasses 3 pints for 1 hundred pounds of meat. This is a simple but excellent recipe.

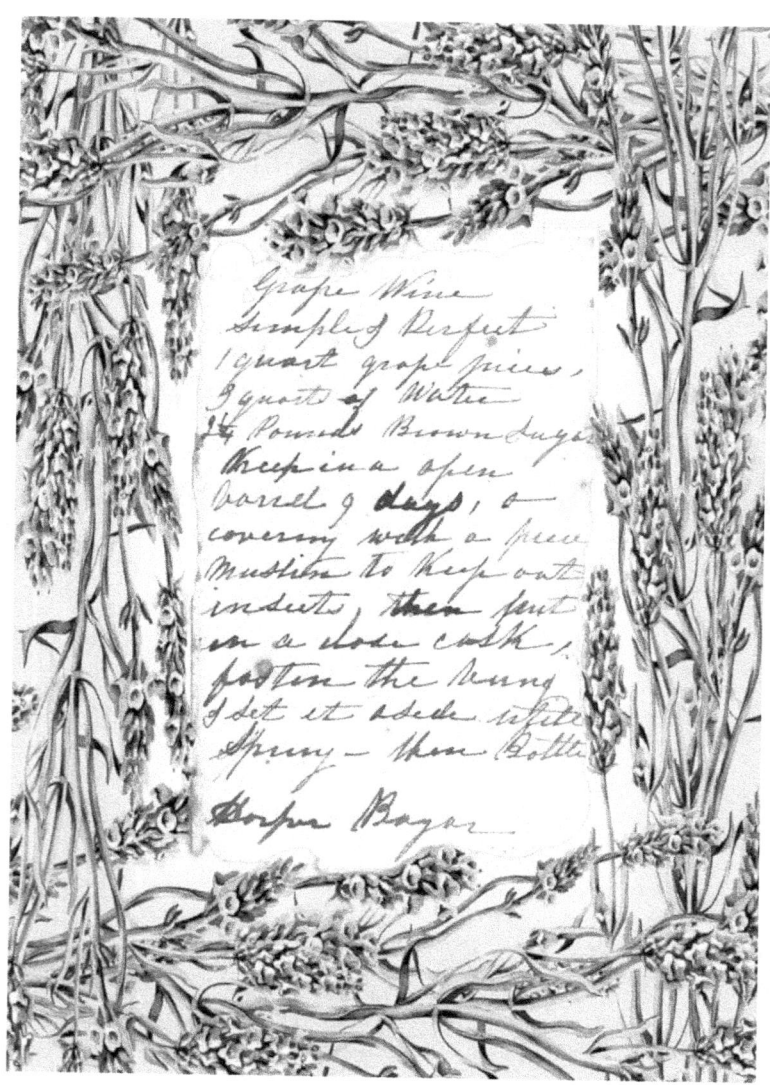

Grape Wine
Simple and Perfect

1 quart of grape juice, 3 quarts of water, 2 ¼ pounds of brown sugar, keep in an open barrel 9 days covering with a piece of muslin to keep out insects, then put in a close cask fasten the rung and set it aside until spring- then bottle

Harpers Bazar

Scotch Short Bread.
Two pounds of flour, one pound of butter, three quarters of a pound of sifted lump sugar, rubbed in three together with the hand, and make into a stiff paste with four eggs, make into square or round cakes; prick the edges. Stick slices of candied peel and some Carraway comfits if liked, on the top, Bake in a ware

Scotch Short Bread

Two pounds of flower, 1 pound of butter, three quarters of pound of sifted lump sugar, rubbed in together with the hand, and make into a stiff paste with four eggs, make into square or round cakes: prick the edges, stick slices of candied peel and some Caraway Comfits, if liked on the top, bake in warm oven on a iron platter.

Soda Biscuit.

To one pint sweet
Milk, add, one teaspoon
subcarbonate of Soda,
2 teaspoonfulls cream a tarter
mixed in the Flour,
A piece of butter the
size of an egg well
rubbed into 1 quart of flour.

Short Biscuit

Half a tb of Butter, ½ tb Sifted
Sugar, 1 Egg, A little Ginger,
And a few Caraway Seeds, with
as much Flour as will make
it into a paste, roll it out
and cut it into Biscuits —

Soda Biscuit

To one pint of sweet milk add, one teaspoonful of subcarbonate of soda, 2 teaspoonfuls cream a tarter mixed in the flour, a piece of butter size of an egg well rubbed into the flour.

Short biscuit

A ½ lb of butter, ½ pound sifted sugar, 1 egg a little ginger and a few caraway seeds, with as much flower and stock making it into a paste, roll it out, and cut it into biscuits.

To Make a Bread Pudding

Make a pint of bread
crumbs, put them in a
stew pan with as much
milk as will cover them,
the peel of a lemon,
a little cinnomon, and
boil them ten minttes,
Sweeten with brown
Sugar take out the
cinnamon, put in
four eggs, beeet all
well togeather, and
bake half a hour,
or boil rather more than
an hour —

To make a Bread pudding

Make a pint of bread crumbs, put them in
a stew pan with as much milk as will
cover them,
the peel of a lemon, a little cinnamon,
and a little nutmeg grated,
boil them ten minutes, with brown sugar
take out the cinnamon, put in four
eggs, beat all well together, and bake
half an hour,
Or
boil rather more than an hour.

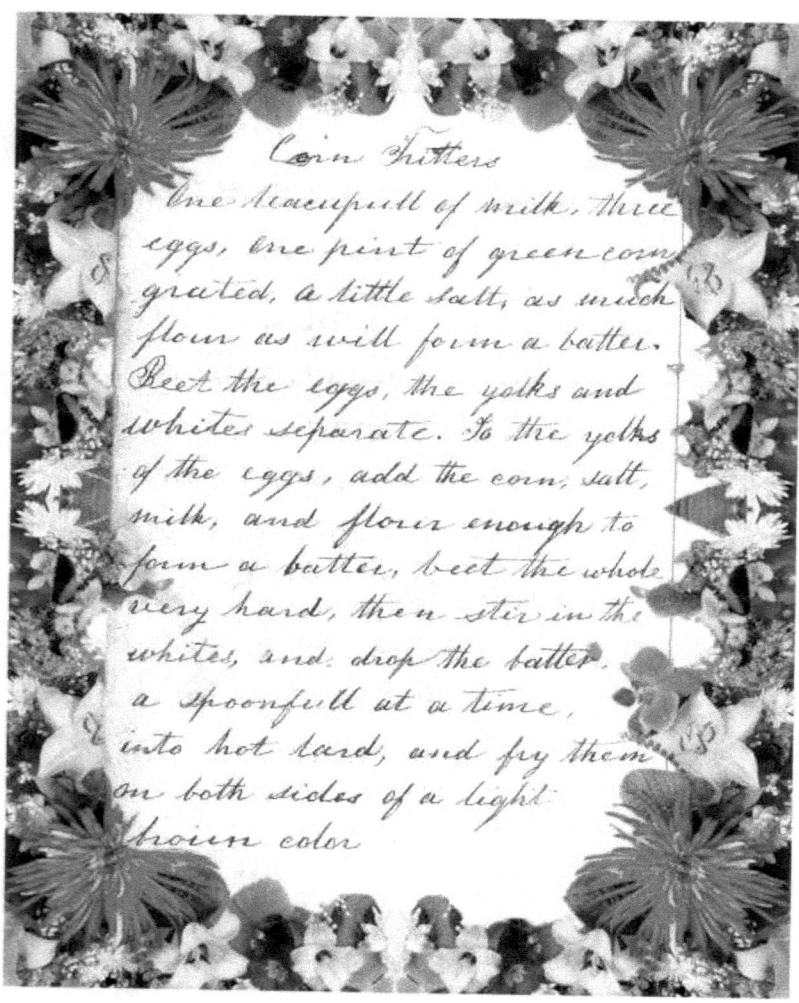

Corn Fritters

One teacupfull of milk, three eggs, one pint of green corn grated, a little salt, as much flour as will form a batter. Beat the eggs, the yolks and whites separate. To the yolks of the eggs, add the corn, salt, milk, and flour enough to form a batter, beat the whole very hard, then stir in the whites, and drop the batter, a spoonfull at a time, into hot lard, and fry them on both sides of a light brown color

Corn fritters

One teacupful of milk, three eggs, one pint of green corn grated, a little salt, as much flour as will form a batter. Beet the eggs, the yolks, and whites separate. To the yolks of the eggs, add the corn, salt, milk, and flour enough to form a batter. beet the whole very hard, then stir in the whites, and drop the batter a spoonful at a time into hot lard, and fry them on both sides of a light brown color.

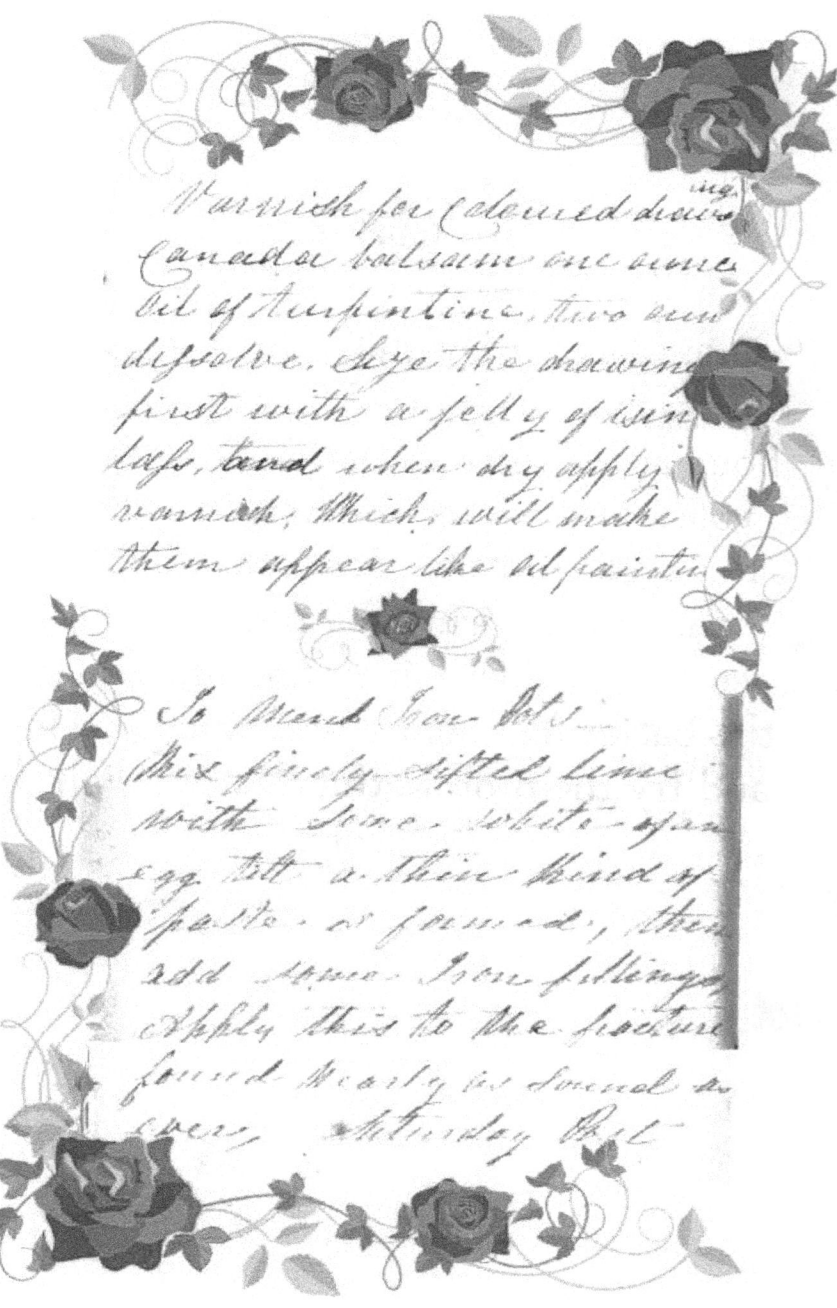

Varnish for Coloured drawing.
Canada balsam one ounce
Oil of Turpintine, two oun[ces]
dissolve. Size the drawing
first with a jelly of isin[g]
lass, and when dry apply
varnish, Which will make
them appear like oil painti[ng]

To Mend Iron Pots
Mix finely sifted lime
with Some white of an
egg till a thin kind of
paste is formed, then
add some Iron filings
Apply this to the fracture
found hearty as sound as
ever. Saturday Post

Varnish for Colored Drawings

Canada balsam one ounce, oil of turpentine, two ounces dissolve, size the drawing first with a jelly of isinglass, and when dry apply varnish, which will make them appear like oil paintings

To mend Iron Pots

Mix some finely sifted lime with some white of an egg till a thin kind of paste is formed, then add some iron fillings. Apply this to the fracture and the vessel will be found nearly as sound as ever.

Saturday Post

Sponge Cake

Beat half a pound of butter to a cream, with a pound of fine white sugar, add half a pint of milk, four well beaten eggs, one wine glass of rose water, a wine glass of brandy, one nutmeg grated, a teaspoonful of ground cinnamon, and half a teaspoonful of saleratus, dissolved in a tablespoonful of hot water, beat in as much wheat flour as will make as thick as pound cake mixture beat well after all line round or square tin pans with buttered paper, put the mixture in an inch deep in square, or an inch and a half in round pans, bake in a quick oven half an hour for square pans, fifty five minutes for round pans. The addition of currants, raisins, and citron, to this cake, makes one which will keep for months, and improve.

Dover Cake

Beat half a pound of butter to a cream, with a pound of fine white sugar, add half a pint of milk, four well beaten eggs, one wine glass of rose water, a wine glass of brandy, one nutmeg grated, a teaspoonful of ground cinnamon, and half a teaspoonful of salaeratus, dissolved in a tablespoon of hot water, beat in as much wheat flour as will make as thick as a pound cake mixture, beat well, after all the ingredients are in, line a round or square tin pan with butter paper, put the mixture an inch deep in square, or an inch and a half in round pans, bake in a quick even half an hour for square pans, forty five for round basins

The addition of currants, raisins, or citron, to this cake, makes one, which will keep for months and improve.

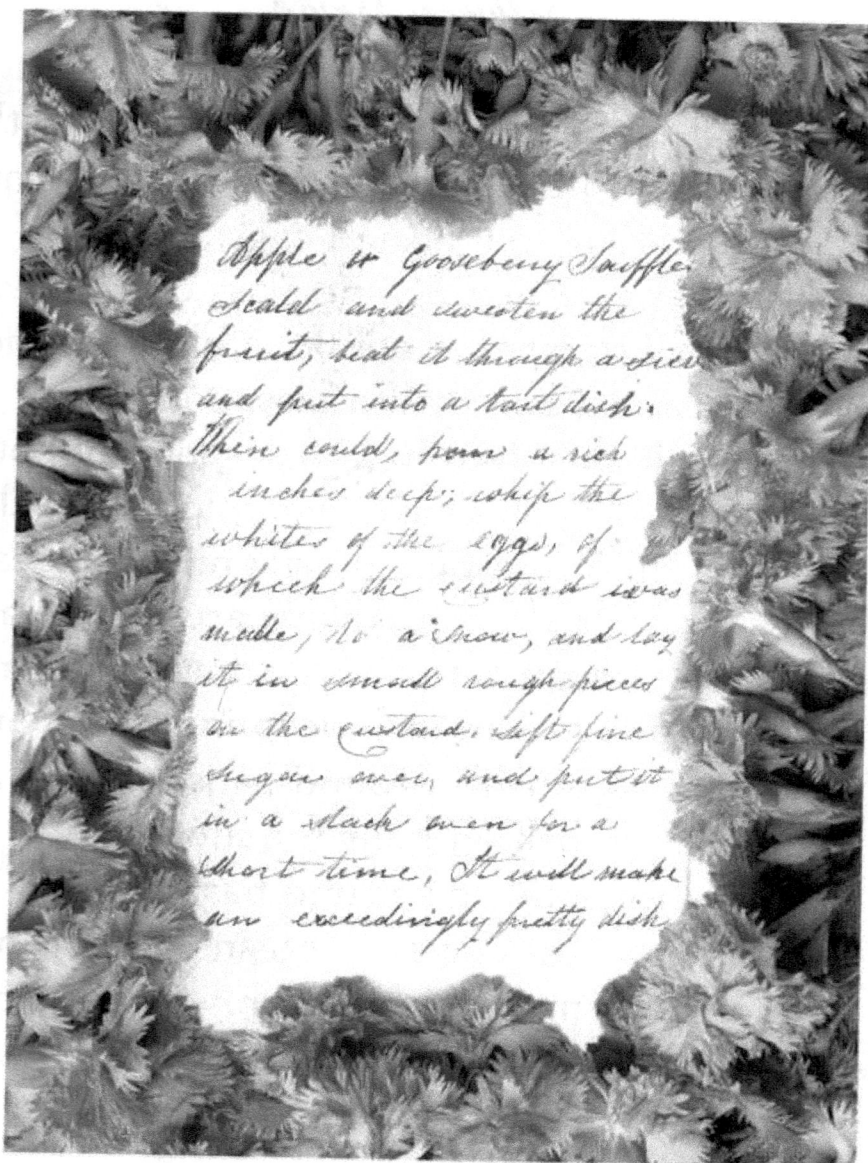

Apple or Gooseberry Souffle.
Scald and sweeten the fruit, beat it through a sieve and put into a tart dish. When cold, pour a rich inches deep; whip the whites of the eggs, of which the custard was made, to a snow, and lay it in small rough pieces on the custard. Sift fine sugar over, and put it in a slack oven for a short time. It will make an exceedingly pretty dish.

Apple or Gooseberry Soufflé

Scald and sweeten the fruit, beat it through a sieve and put it in a tart dish. When cold pour a rich custard over it, about two inches deep; whip the whites of the eggs of which the custard was made, to a snow and lay it in small rough pieces on the custard, sift fine sugar over. and put in a slack oven for a short time, It will make an exceedingly pretty dish.

To Color Green
To 4 ths. of fustick take
1 tts of logwood chips—
(not the extract) and
once oz of vitriol, Boil
the wood until the
strength is obtained,
then add the vitriol,
This solution will
color 4 or 5 tts of goods.
put in the goods and boil
10 or 15 minutes, have
ready hot ~~soap~~ suds
and wash just as soon
as drained, Do not rinse
it after washing in
the suds

To color Green

To 4 lbs of fustick take 1 lb of logwood chips (not the extract) and one oz of vitriol boil the wood until the strength is obtained, then add the vitriol. This solution will color 4 or 5 lbs of goods. Put in the goods and boil 10 or 15 minutes, have ready pot soapsuds and wash just as soon as drained, do not rinse it after washing in the suds.

Rural New Yorker

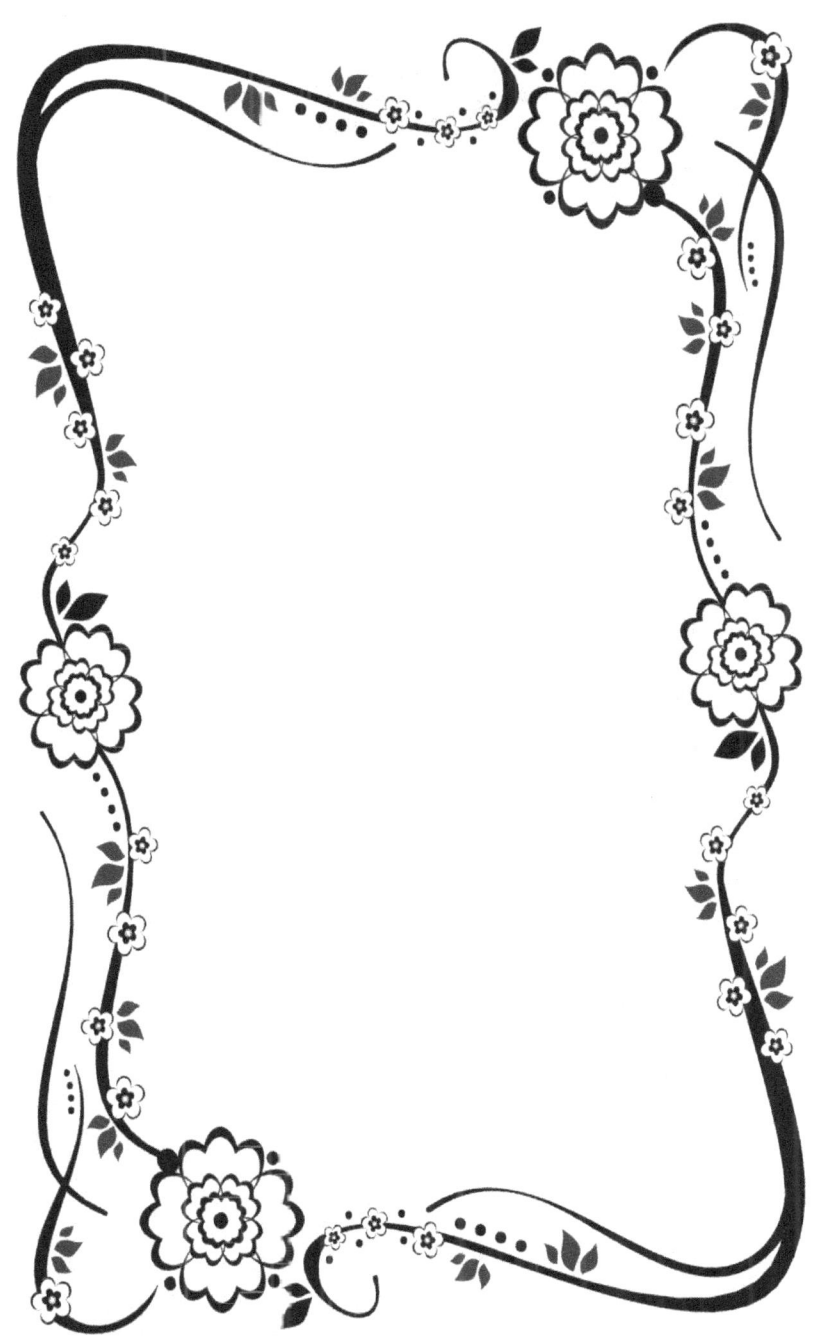

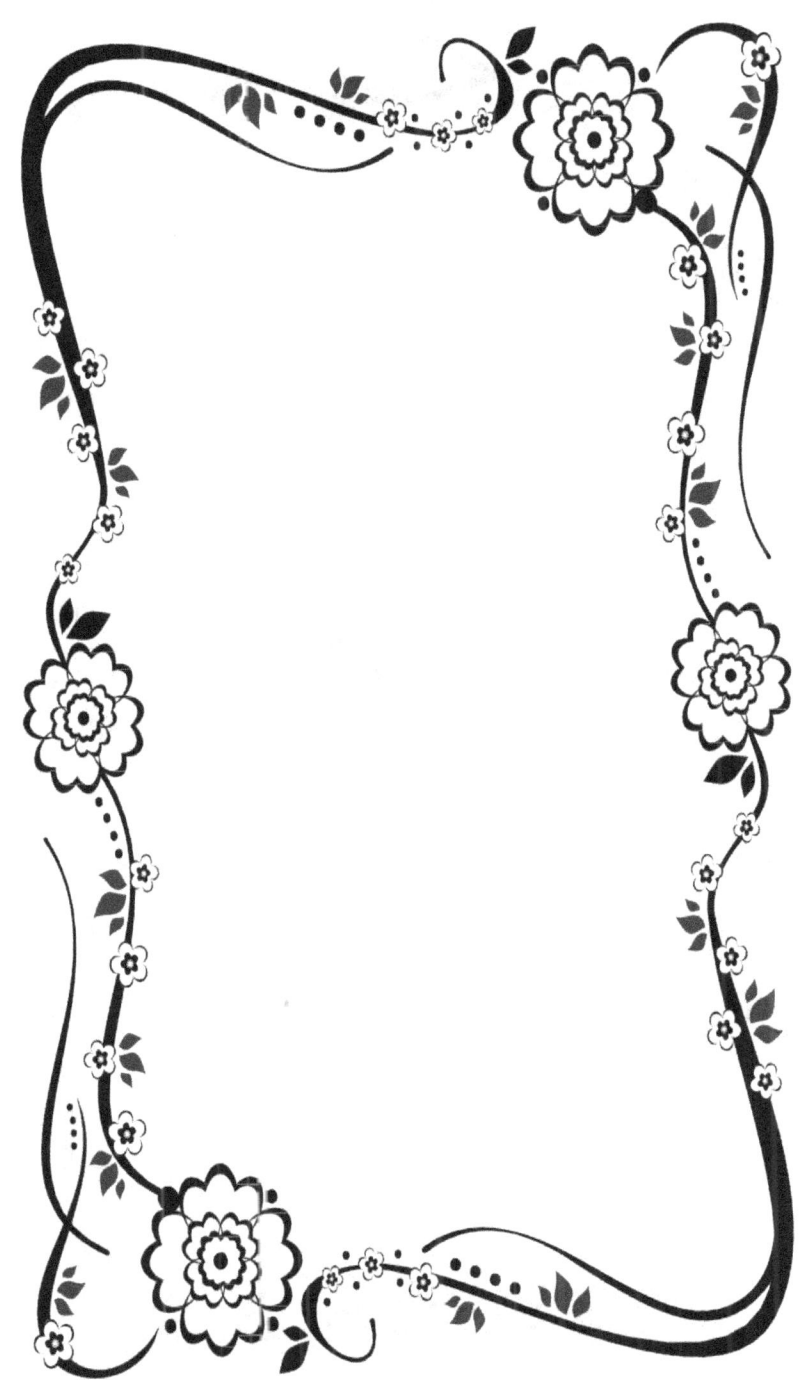

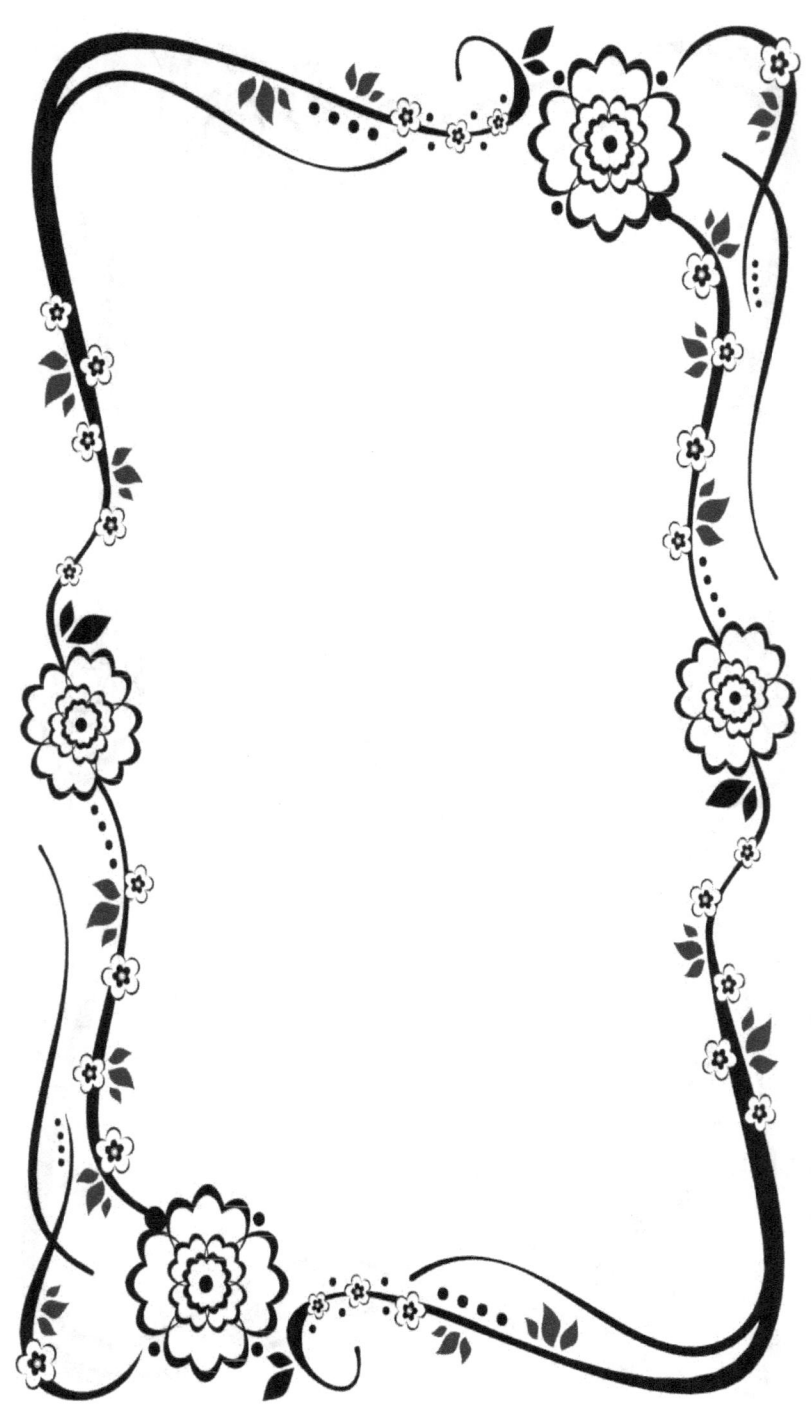

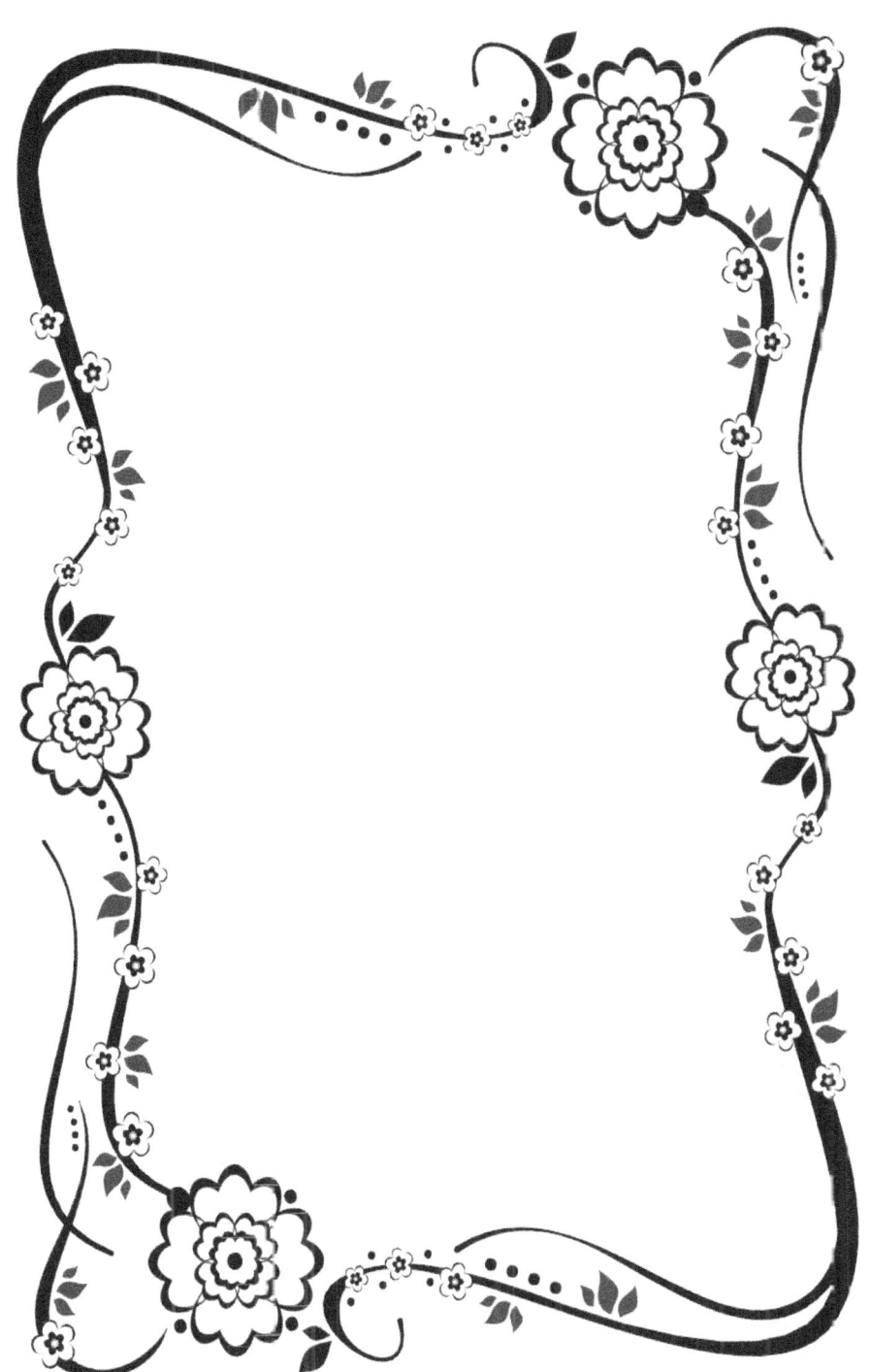

Culinary Measurements

Teaspoon	Tablespoon	Cup	Pint	Quart	Gallon	Fluid Ounces	Metric
1/8	-	-	-	-	-	-	1/2 ml
1/4	-	-	-	-	-	-	1 ml
1/2	1/6	-	-	-	-	-	2 ml
1	1/3	-	-	-	-	-	5 ml
3	1	1/16	-	-	-	1/2	15 ml
6	2	1/8	-	-	-	1	30 ml
12	4	1/4	-	-	-	2	60 ml
16	5 1/3	1/3	-	-	-	2 2/3	80 ml
-	8	1/2	1/4	-	-	4	125 ml
-	16	1	1/2	1/4	-	8	250 ml
-	-	2	1	1/2	-	16	500 ml OR 1/2 liter
-	-	3	1-1/2	3/4	-	24	750 ml (s]td, wine bottle)
-	-	4	2	1	¼	32	1 liter
-	-	8	4	2	1/2	64	2 liters
-	-	16	8	4	1	128	4 liters

TEMPERATURES	
Very slow oven	Below 300 degrees F
Slow oven	300 degrees F
Moderately slow oven	325 degrees F
Moderate oven	350 degrees F
Moderately hot oven	375 degrees F
Quick oven	375-400 degrees F
Hot oven	400-425 degrees F
Very hot oven	450-475 degrees F
Extremely hot oven	500 degrees F or more

MEASUREMENTS	
1 Wineglass	1/4 Cup
1 Jigger	1.5 Fluid Ounces
1 Gill	1/2 Cup
1 Teacup	A Scant 3/4 Cup
1 Coffee Cup	A Scant Cup
1 Tumbler	1 Cup
1 Pint	2 Cups
1 Quart	4 Cups
1 Peck	2 Gallons – Dry
1 Pinch or Dash	What can be picked up between thumb and
1 Nickel	first two fingers; Less than 1/8 teaspoon size of a nickel in the palm of a hand
1/2 Pinch	What can be picked up between the thumb and one finger
1 Saltspoon	1/4 Teaspoon
1 Kitchen Spoon	1 Teaspoon
1 Dessert Spoon	2 Teaspoons **or** 1 Soupspoon
1 Spoonful	1 Tablespoon more or less
1 Saucer	1 Heaping Cup (About)

COMMON WEIGHTS	
1 Penny Weight	1/20 Ounce
1 Drachm	1/8 Ounce
60 Drops Thick Fluid	1 Teaspoon
1 Ounce	4-1/2 Tablespoons, Allspice, Cinnamon, Curry, Paprika, or Dry Mustard; **Or** 4 Tablespoons Cloves or Prepared Mustard; **Or** 3-1/2 Tablespoons Nutmeg or Pepper **Or** 3 Tablespoons Sage, Cream of Tarter or Cornstarch; **Or** 2 Tablespoons Salt or Any Liquid

COMMON WEIGHTS	
1 Pound	2 Cups liquid; Or 4 Cups Flour; Or 8 Medium Eggs with Shells; Or 10 Eggs Without Shells; Or 2 Cups Granulated Sugar; Or 2-1/3 Cups Packed Brown Sugar; Or 3-3/4 Cups Unsifted Confectioner's Sugar; Or 4-1/2 Cups Sifted Confectioner's Sugar; Or 4 Cups Grated Cabbage, Cranberries, Coffee or Chopped Celery; Or 3 Cups Corn Meal; Or 2 Cups Uncooked Rice; Or 2-3/4 Cups Raisins or Dried Currants

COMMON WEIGHTS	
Butter the Size of an Egg	1/4 Cup or 2 Ounces
Butter the Size of a Walnut	1 Tablespoon
Butter the Size of a Hazlenut	1 Teaspoon

Short Histories of Culinary Functions

Butter: its History and a Little Folklore

First churned some say almost 4000 years ago, butter became a basic and significant staple. Folklore has it, one hot day when a traveler tied a container full of milk to his luggage being carried by his horse, found at the end of the day the heat and movement had churned the milk to a tasty yellow item for consumption. Before butter became exclusively a food, it was used as money or for barter. It's said that early settlers from Europe stored the precious cargo on the ships that sailed to the New World.

The norm for many years was to produce butter at home. The homemaker would take cream and speedily mix to form butter lumps, as they continued to mix (churn) the butter became thicker, which produced a liquid referred to as liquid buttermilk. The continuing process was to draw off the buttermilk, that is when the butter was washed and either used or stored. Churns evolved from skin pouches to earthenware pots, which were rocked, shaken or swung to separate the fat. Later, the dasher, a wooden stick with a blunt end was used to churn butter in a conical wooden vessel. Eventually modern production techniques developed glass and metal churns.

When the washed butter was removed from the churn in the olden days, it was placed into a "butter" bowl to be weighed. Paddles were used to remove the butter from the flat wooden bowl and to shape butter balls. Or, the butter was placed in a specially designed mold, usually a family's treasured possession, or formed into rolls or blocks. If the butter was to be stored for later use, salt was worked into the mixture and the butter packed into molds or tubs and stored in water crocks in the family well.

In 1848, after being a family owned business with local butter distributed through country stores, the first butter factory was established near Goshen, New York. Farmers brought their milk to this receiving station to sell it for conversion to butter. From that small beginning, the butter industry spread to become a vital part of the dairy industry. Butter has been the basis for naming characters in plays and comic strips, for identifying a specific color or song, as a colloquial term and rule of behavior: for example, "buttering up" your boss for a raise; "knowing which side your bread is buttered on": writing a "bread and butter 'thank you' letter."

For thousands of years mankind thrived on butter. It has been eaten alone, drunk in tea, spread on almost every other food, cooked with innumerable foods and seasonings. It has been used as a medicine, a hair dressing, oil, a poultice to erase wrinkles and as a means for buying a wife. Yet modern butter, manufactured and processed by scientific methods, has not really changed from the earliest product.

Quince - Cultural Associations

In Turkey, the expression (ayvayi yemek) (literally: to eat quince) is used as a derogatory term indicating any unpleasant situation or a malevolent incident to avoid. This usage is likened to the rather bitter aftertaste of a quince fruit inside the mouth.

When a baby is born in Slavonia (Croatia), a quince tree is planted as a symbol of fertility, love and life.

Ancient Greek poets (Ibycus, Aristophanes, e.g.) used quinces (kydonia) as a mildly ribald term for teenage breasts.

Although the book of Genesis does not name the specific type of the fruit that Adam and Eve ate from the tree of knowledge of good and evil in the garden of Eden, some ancient texts suggest Eve's fruit of temptation might have been a quince.

In Plutarch's Lives, Solon is said to have decreed that "bride and bridegroom shall be shut into a chamber, and eat a quince together."

Toxicology

The seeds contain nitriles, which are common in seeds of the rose family. In the stomach, enzymes or stomach acid or both cause some of the nitriles to be hydrolyzed and produce hydrogen cyanide, which is a volatile gas. The seeds are only likely to be toxic if a large quantity is eaten.
In Lebanon and Syria, it is called *sfarjel* and also used to make jam- Mrabba sfarjal. In Syria, quince is cooked in pomegranate paste (dibs rouman) with shank meat and kibbeh (a Middle Eastern meat pie with burghul and mince meat) and is called *kibbeh safarjalieh.* In Pakistan, quinces are stewed with sugar until they turn bright red. The resulting stewed quince, called *muraba* is then preserved in jars and eaten like jam. In Morocco, when the fruit is available, it is a popular ingredient in a seasonal lamb tajine and is cooked together with the meat and flavoured with cinnamon and other herbs and spices.

In Argentina, Chile, Mexico, Spain, Peru, Uruguay and Venezuela, the *membrillo*, as the quince is called in Spanish, is cooked into a reddish, jelly-like block or firm, reddish paste known as *dulce de membrillo*. It is then eaten in sandwiches and with cheese, traditionally manchego cheese, or accompanying fresh curds. In Portugal, a similar sweet is called *marmelada*, hince marmalade in English. It is also produced and consumed in Hungary, where it is called *birsalmasajt*, "quince cheese". The sweet and floral notes of *carne de membrillo* (quince meat) contrast nicely with the tanginess of the cheese. Boiled quince is also popular in desserts such as the *murta con membrillo* that combines *Ugni molinae* with quince. Similar dishes exist in Dalmatia and other parts of Croatia.

In the Alsace region of France and the Valais region of Switzerland, *liqueur de coing* made from quince is used as a *digestif*.

In Morocco green quince is cooked in a tajine with beef or lamb, sweetened slightly with sugar and flavored with cinnamon.

Quince can also be used as a tea additive to mainly green tea, giving it a rather sweetish taste.

In Kashmir quince is cooked with lamb and served in weddings to guests.

In Taiwan yellow quinces are often confused with pomelos.

In Tajikistan, quince is used in cooking oshi palov. Quince jam is known as murabboi bihigi, and also made in many parts of the country.
Most varieties of quince are too hard, astringent and sour to eat raw unless 'bletted' (softened by frost and subsequent decay). High in pectin, they are used to make jam, jelly and quince pudding, or they may be peeled, then roasted, baked or stewed. The pectin level diminishes as they ripen. The flesh of the fruit turns red after a long cooking time. The very strong perfume means they can be added in small quantities to apple pies and jam to enhance the flavour.

Adding a diced quince to apple sauce will enhance the taste of the apple sauce with the chunks of relatively firm, tart quince. The term "marmalade," originally meaning a quince jam, derives from "marmelo," the Portuguese word for this fruit.

The fruit, like so many others, can be used to make a type of wine. Because of its often high acidity, which is mainly due to its malic acid content, these wines are usually sweet dessert wines that are high in alcohol. In the Balkans and elsewhere, quince brandy and quince liqueur are made. In Carolina in 1709, John Lawson allowed that he was "not a fair judge of the different sorts of quinces, which they call Brunswick, Portugal and Barbary," but he noted "of this fruit they make a wine or liquor which they call Quince-Drink, and which I approve of beyond any that their country affords, though a great deal of cider and perry is there made, the Quince-Drink most commonly purges."
Varieties of quince, such as 'Kuganskaya,' have been developed that do not require cooking and are eaten raw.

In Iran, quince, called *beh*, is used raw or in stews and some regional soups. It is also made into jam or preserve. The extra syrup in the jam making process is saved and made into a refreshing summer drink by adding cold water and a few drops of lime to it. It can also be found pickled.

In Italy, it is used as the main ingredient of some local variants of a traditional food called mostarda (not to be confused with mustard), in which quince fruit jam is mixed with candied fruit, spices and flavorings to produce a spread that is used on boiled meat, mixed with cheese etc. Examples are "mostarda vicentina" or "mostarda di Vicenza" and "mostarda veneta." Quinces are also used in Parma to produce a typical liqueur called sburlone, word coming from the local dialect and meaning the necessary high stress to squeeze those hard fruits to obtain their juice. In Albania, Kosovo and Bulgaria quince are eaten raw during the winter.

Glossary

Terminology Used in Recipes from the 1700's - 1800's

ISINGLASS
1. A semitransparent whitish very pure gelatin prepared from the air bladders of fishes (as sturgeons) and used especially as a clarifying agent and in jellies and glue
2. **Mica** especially when in thin transparent sheets; *especially*: MUSCOVITE *First known use: 1535*

Salaerutus   baking soda
Noun: a white soluble compound (NaHCO3) used in effervescent drinks and in baking powders and as an antacid

What is rennet?
Traditional animal rennet is an enzyme derived from the stomachs of calves, lambs or goats before they consume anything but milk.
Vegetable rennet is obtained from a type of mold (Mucur Meithei). However, even though it is derived from mold, there is no mold contained in the final product. It is an equivalent chymosin product, which works equally well but is not animal derived. Rennet thrives at temperatures in the 85-105F range, but it will not be deactivated completely until it reaches the 140F's. Rennet continues working to set the milk as long as it has the right conditions. So, when a recipe calls for cutting the curds after a certain time period, it is important to follow the directions. Otherwise, your curds may be too firm for the cheese you are trying to make.

Lawn cloth or lawn is plain weave textile, originally of linen but now chiefly cotton. Lawn is designed using fine, high-count yarns, which results in a silky, untextured feel. The fabric is made using either combed or carded yarns. When lawn is made using combed yarns, with a soft feel and slight luster, it is known as "nainsook". The term lawn is also used in the textile industry to refer to a type of starched crisp finish given to a cloth product. The finish can be applied to a variety of fine fabrics, prints, or plain. Lawn is a lightweight, sheer cloth, crisper than voile, but not as crisp as organdy. Lawn is known for its semi-transparency, which can range from gauzy or sheer to an almost opaque effect, known as lining or utility lawn. The finish used on lawn ranges from soft to semi-crisp to crisp, but the fabric is never completely stiff. Lawn can be white, or may be dyed or printed.

Demijohn
A large bottle with a short narrow neck, often with small handles at the neck and encased in wickerwork

Pally Pans

Caisse Pan Dish similar to those that casseroles are made

Treacle Molasses (American & Canadian English), is any uncrystallized **syrup** made during the refining of **sugar**. Treacle is used both in cooking as a sweetener and as a **condiment**.

Salt petre Potassium nitrate is a **chemical compound** with the **formula KNO**$_3$. It is an **ionic salt** of **potassium ions** K^+ and **nitrate ions** NO_3^-. It occurs as a mineral **niter** and is a natural solid source of **nitrogen**. Potassium nitrate is one of several nitrogen-containing compounds collectively referred to as **saltpeter** or salt petre. Major uses of potassium nitrate are in fertilizers, **rocket propellants** and **fireworks**. It is one of the major constituents of **gunpowder** (blackpowder) and has been used since the Middle Ages as a food preservative.

Pearl Ash Potassium carbonate was first identified in 1742 by Antonio Campanella and is the primary component of potash and the more refined pearl ash or salts of tartar.

Fustic Is a common name for several plants and a dye produced from these plants:

Drachm (fluid):
Unit of volume, equal to 60 minims. 8 fluid drachms to the fluid ounce.

www.ingramcontent.com/pod-product-compliance
Lightning Source LLC
Chambersburg PA
CBHW070844160426
43192CB00012B/2297